SWEAR & COLORS

SWEAR WORD COLORING BOOK TO RELIEF ANGER AND STRESS

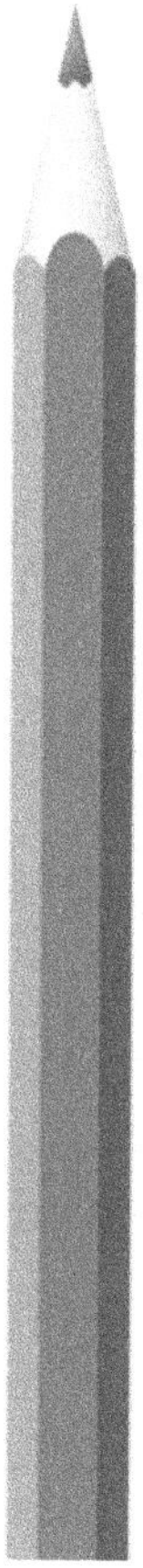

COLOR TEST PAGE

SWEAR &
COLORS

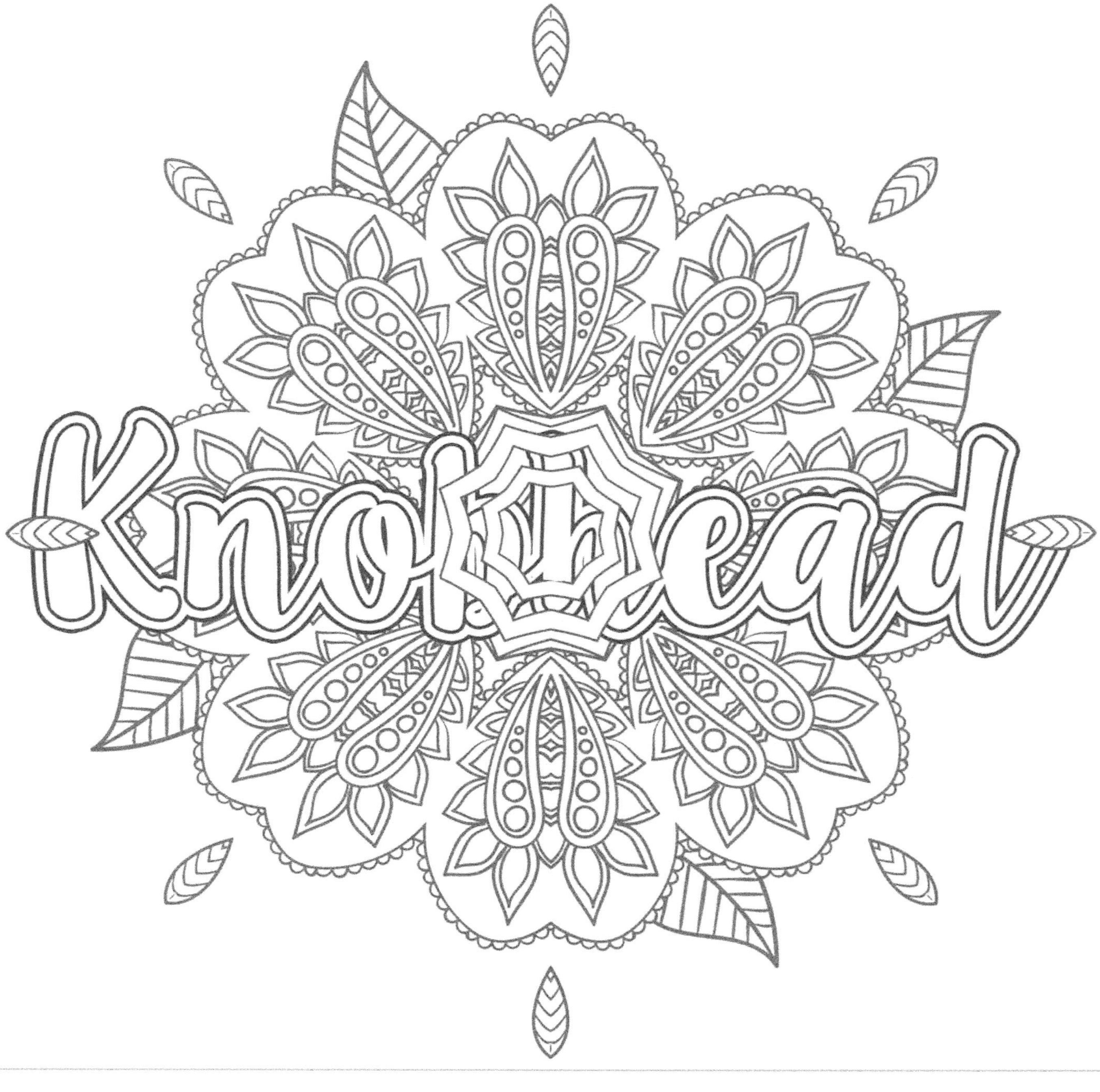
Knobhead

SWEAR & COLORS

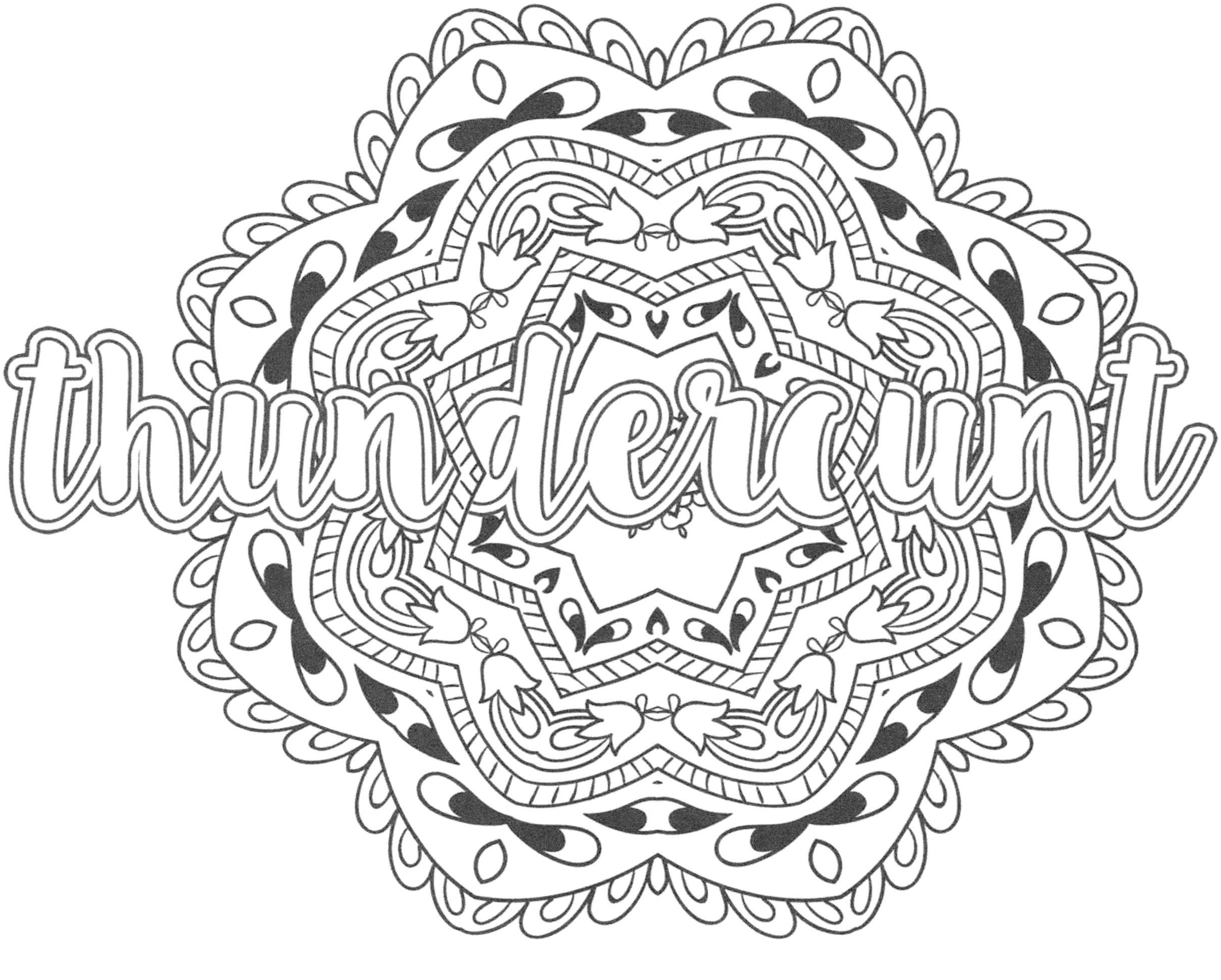
thundercunt

SWEAR &
COLORS

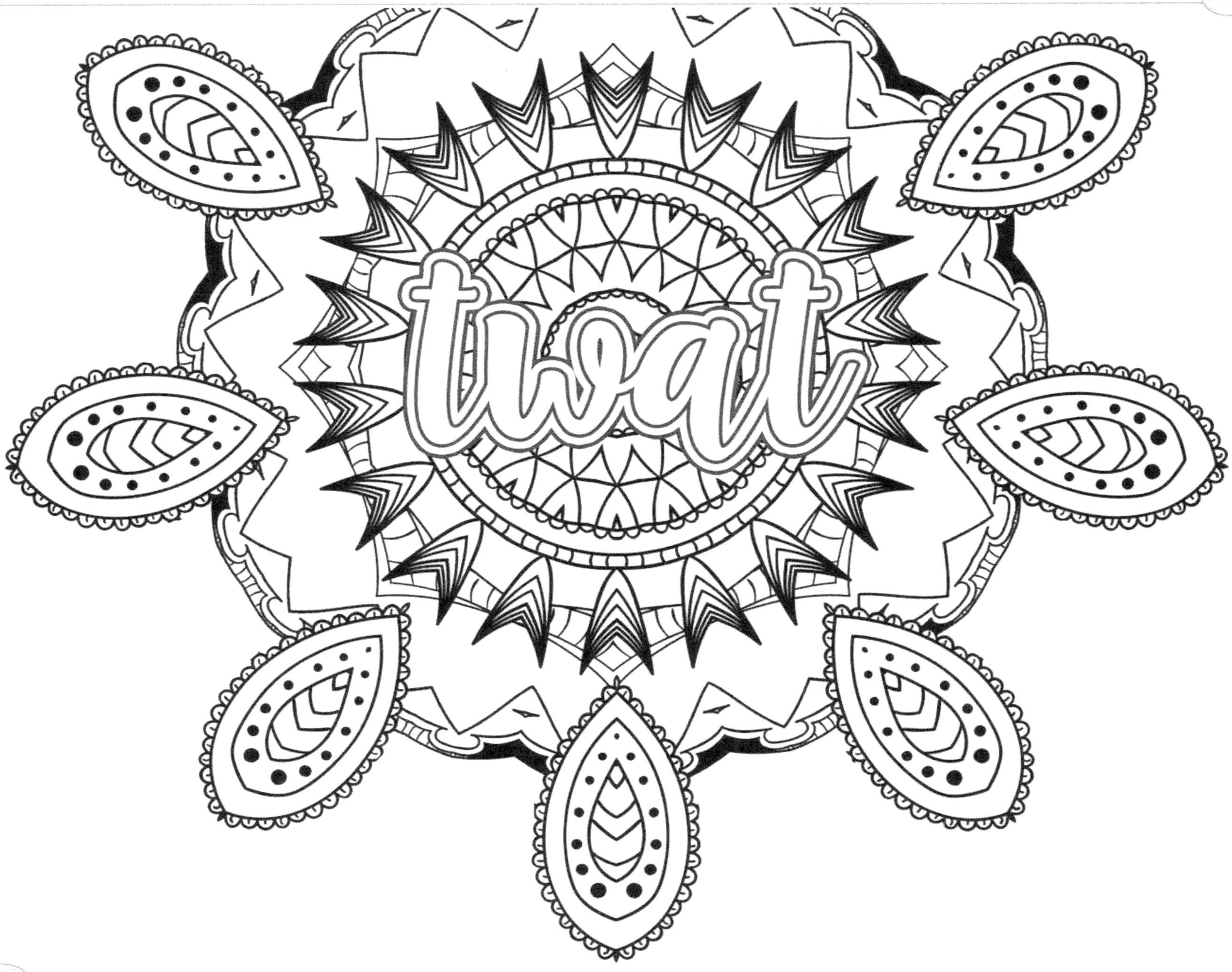
twat

SWEAR & COLORS

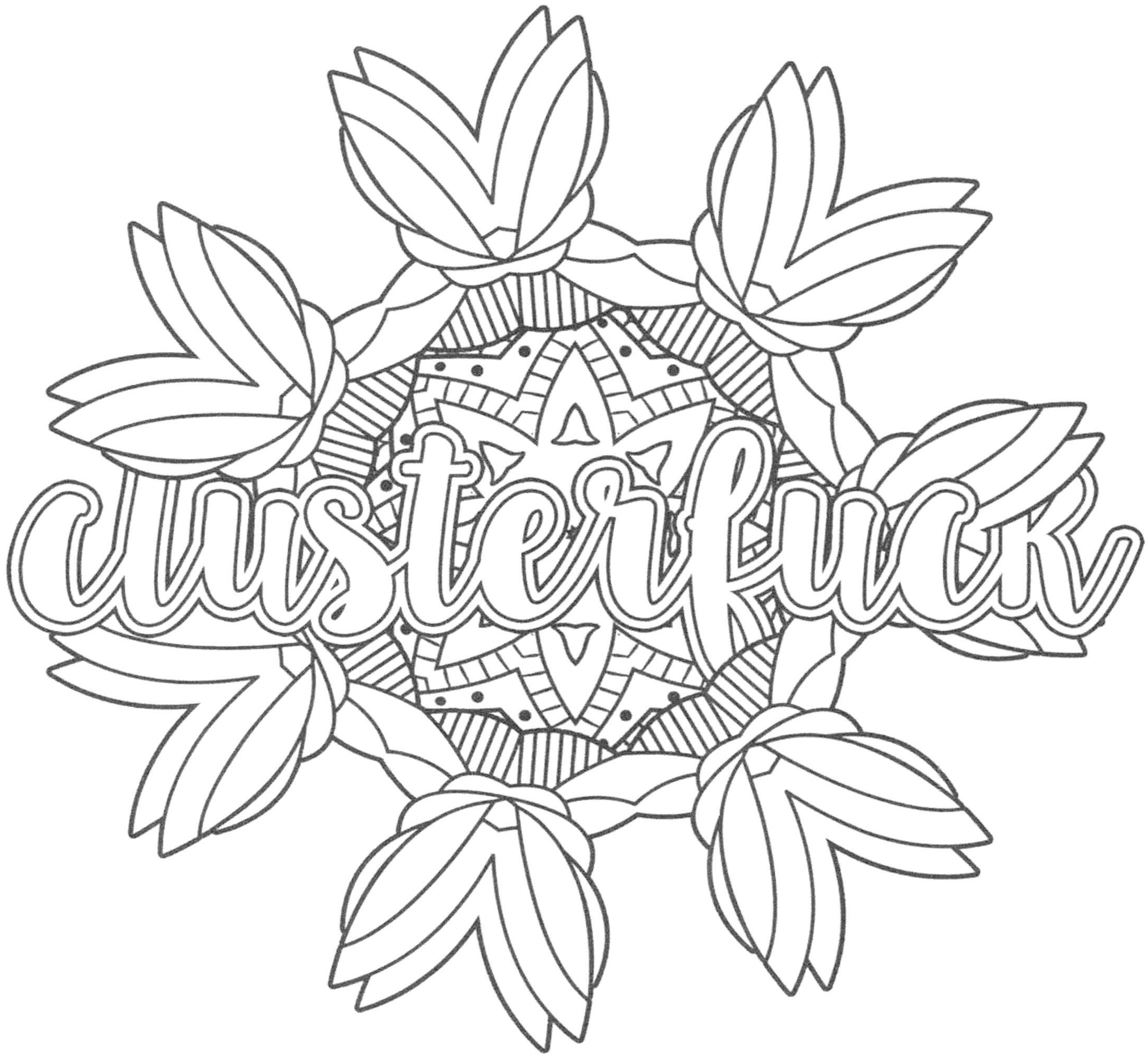
clusterfuck

SWEAR &
COLORS

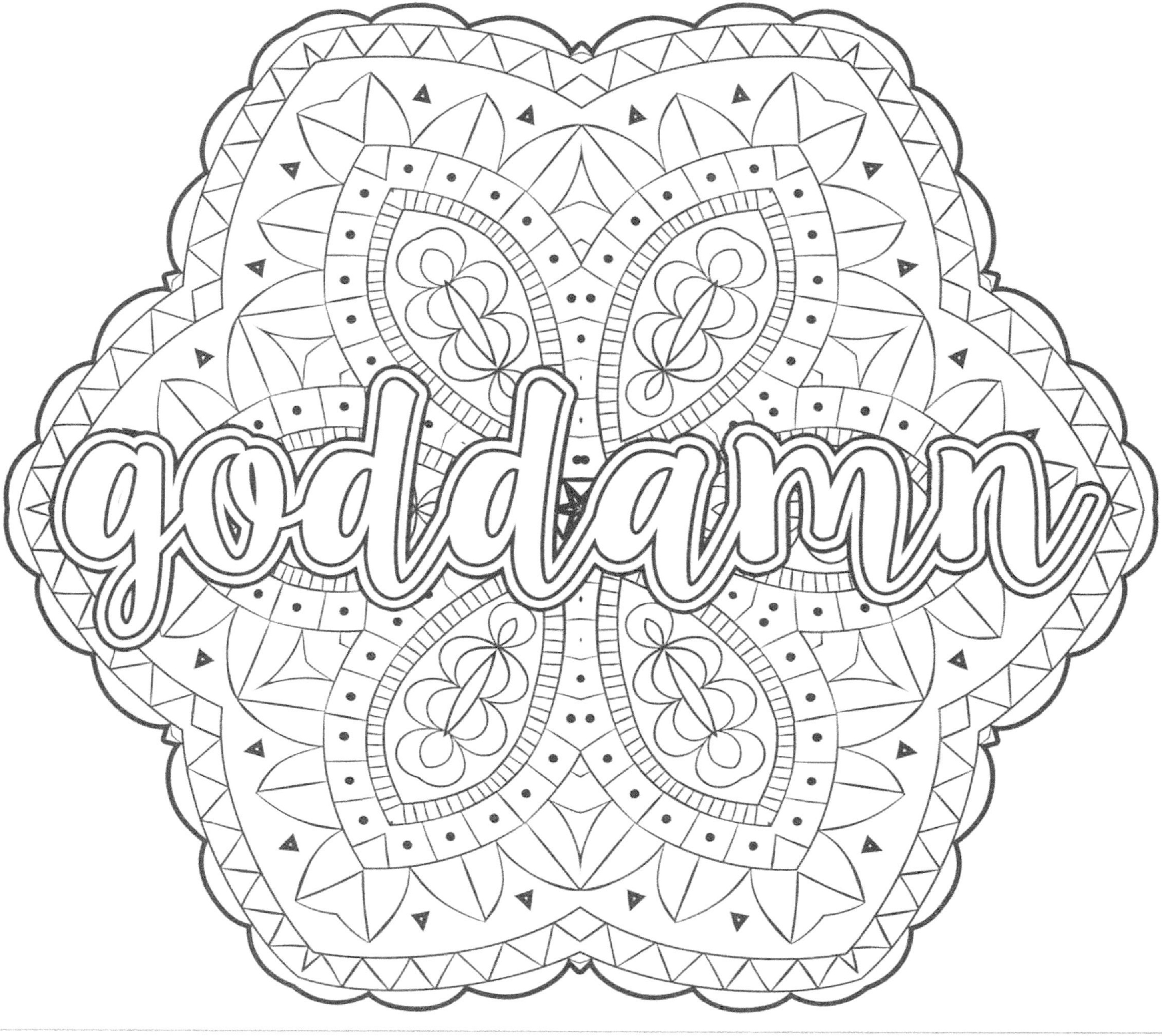
goddamn

SWEAR & COLORS

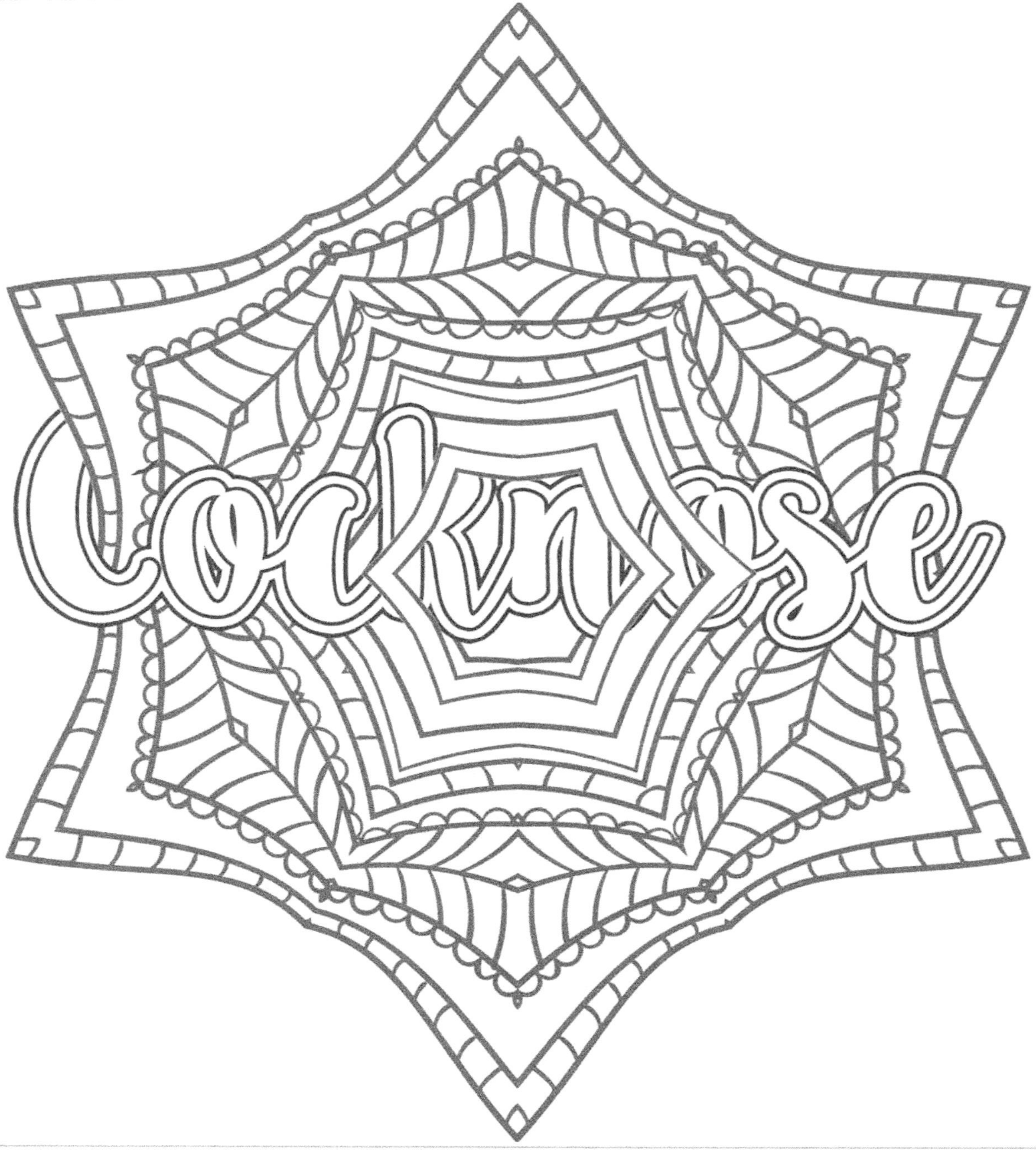
Cocknose

SWEAR & COLORS

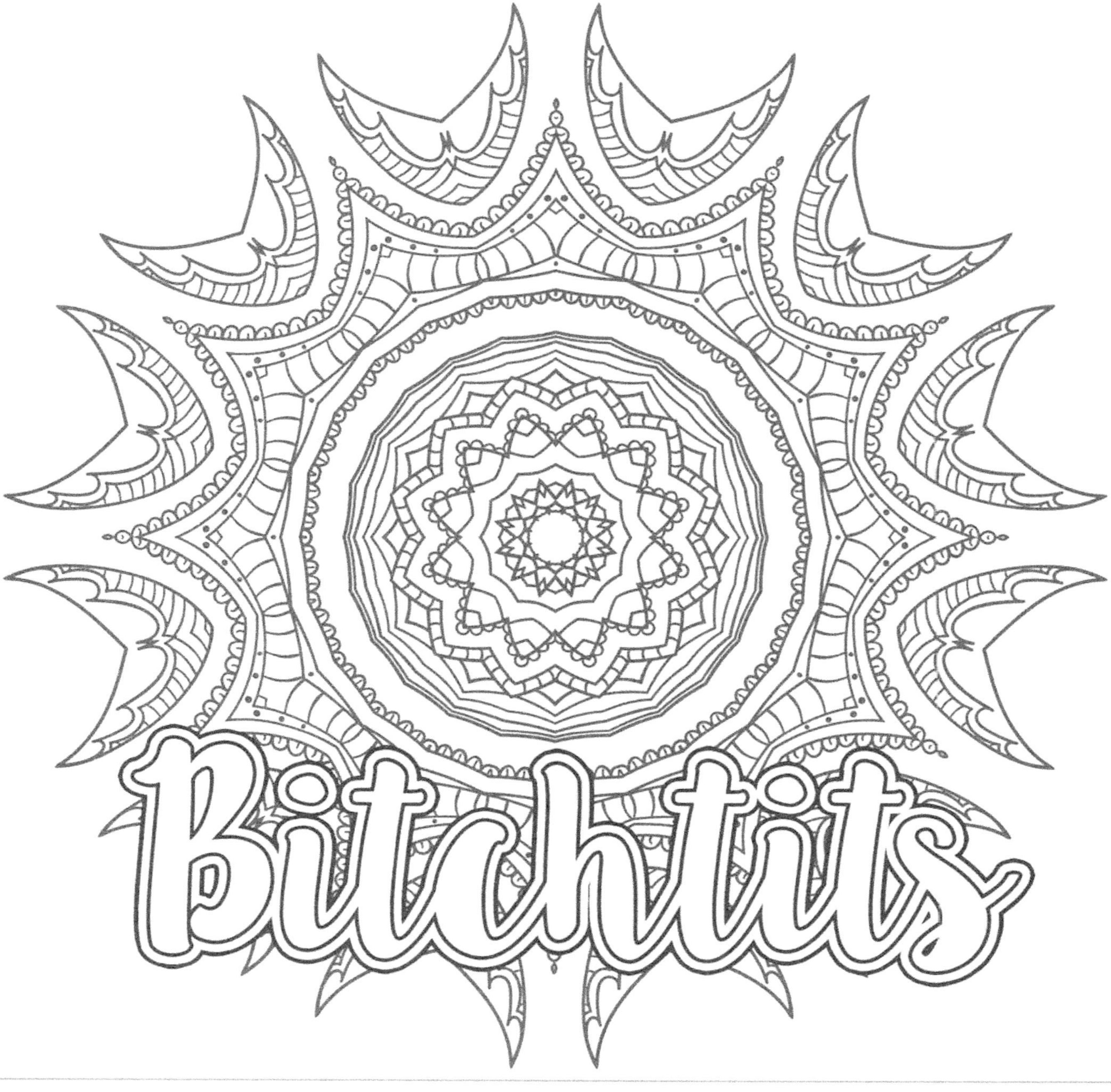
Bitchtits

SWEAR &
COLORS

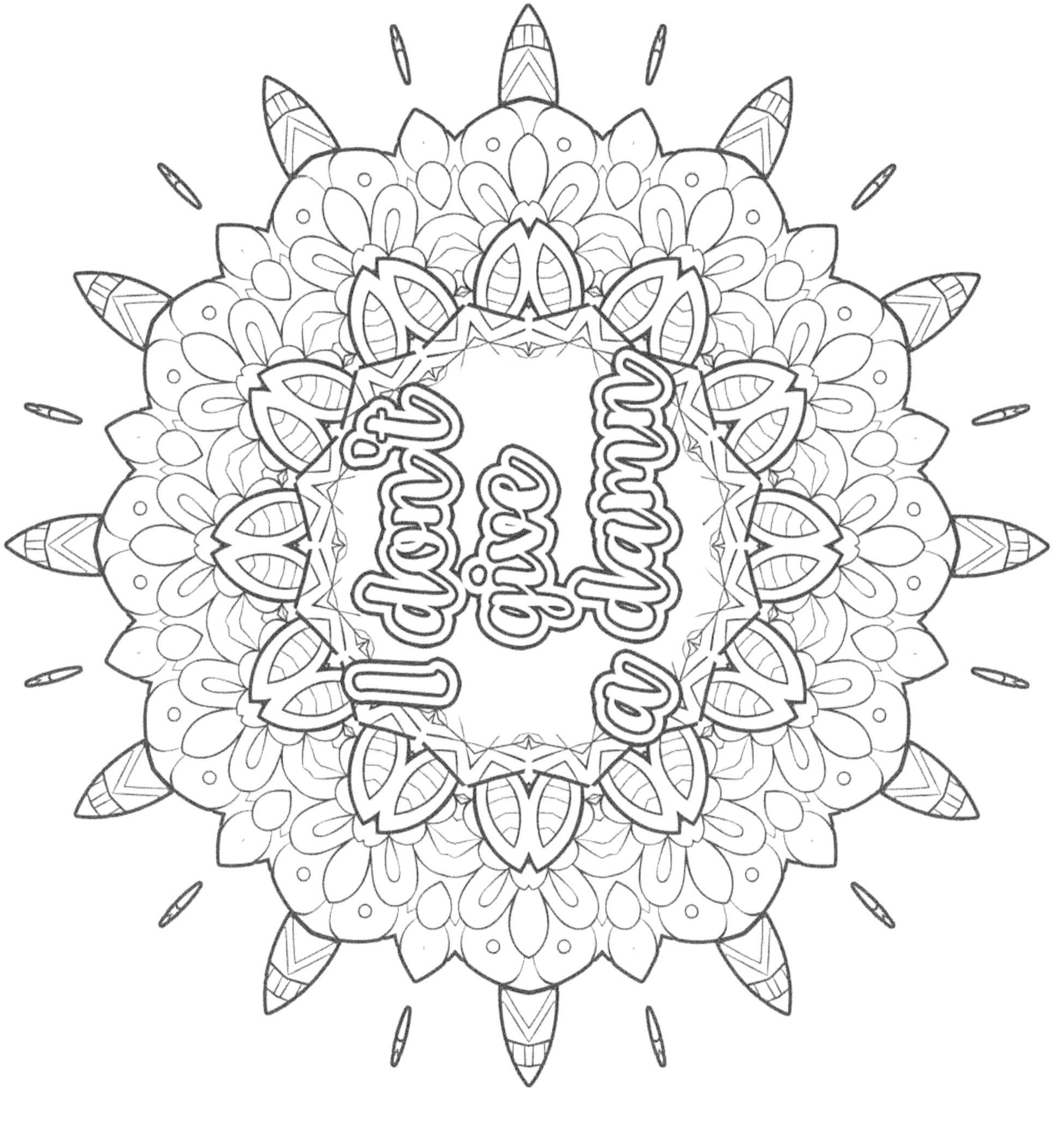
I don't give a damn

SWEAR &
COLORS

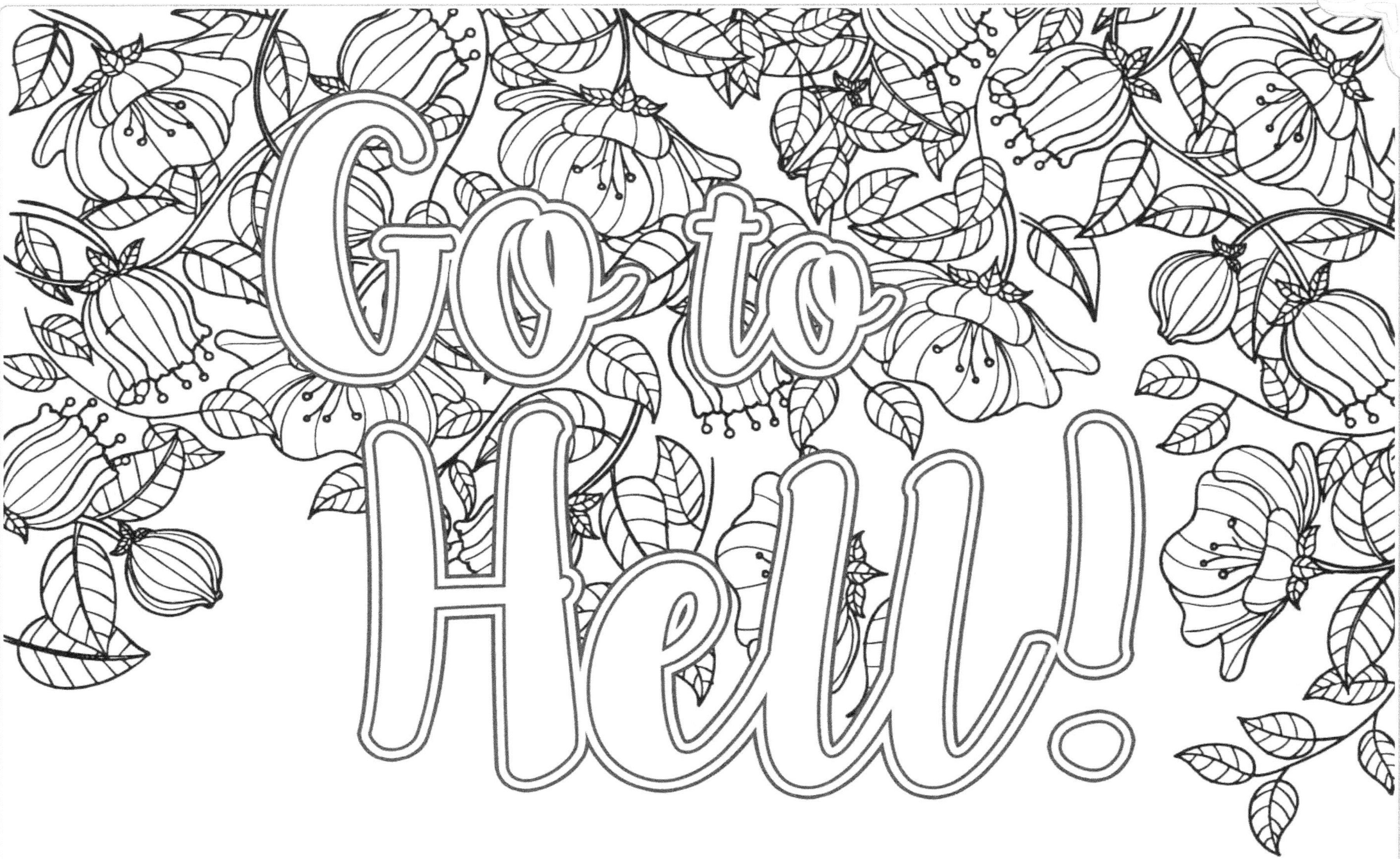
Go to
Hell!

SWEAR & COLORS

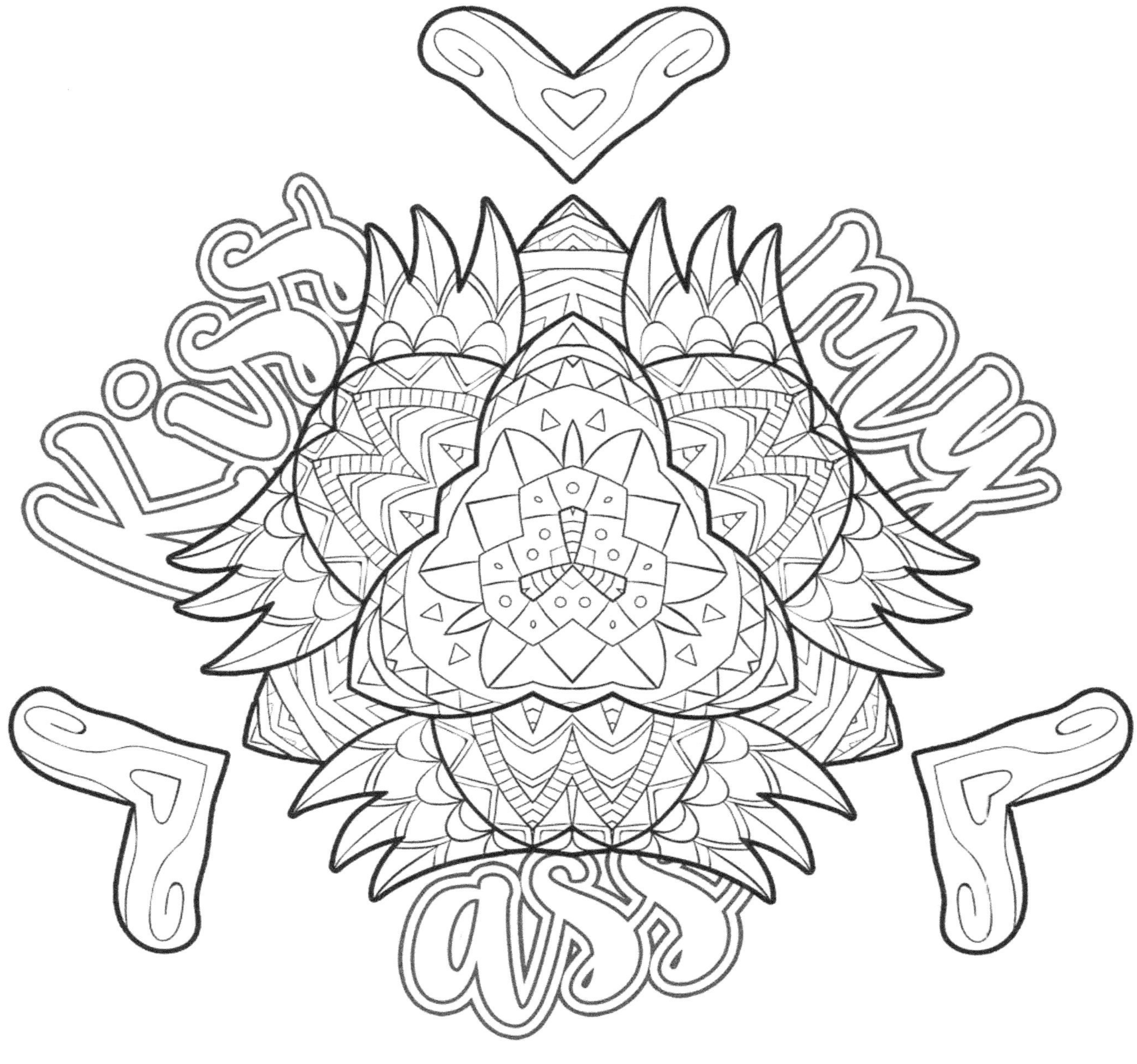
kiss my
ass

SWEAR &
COLORS

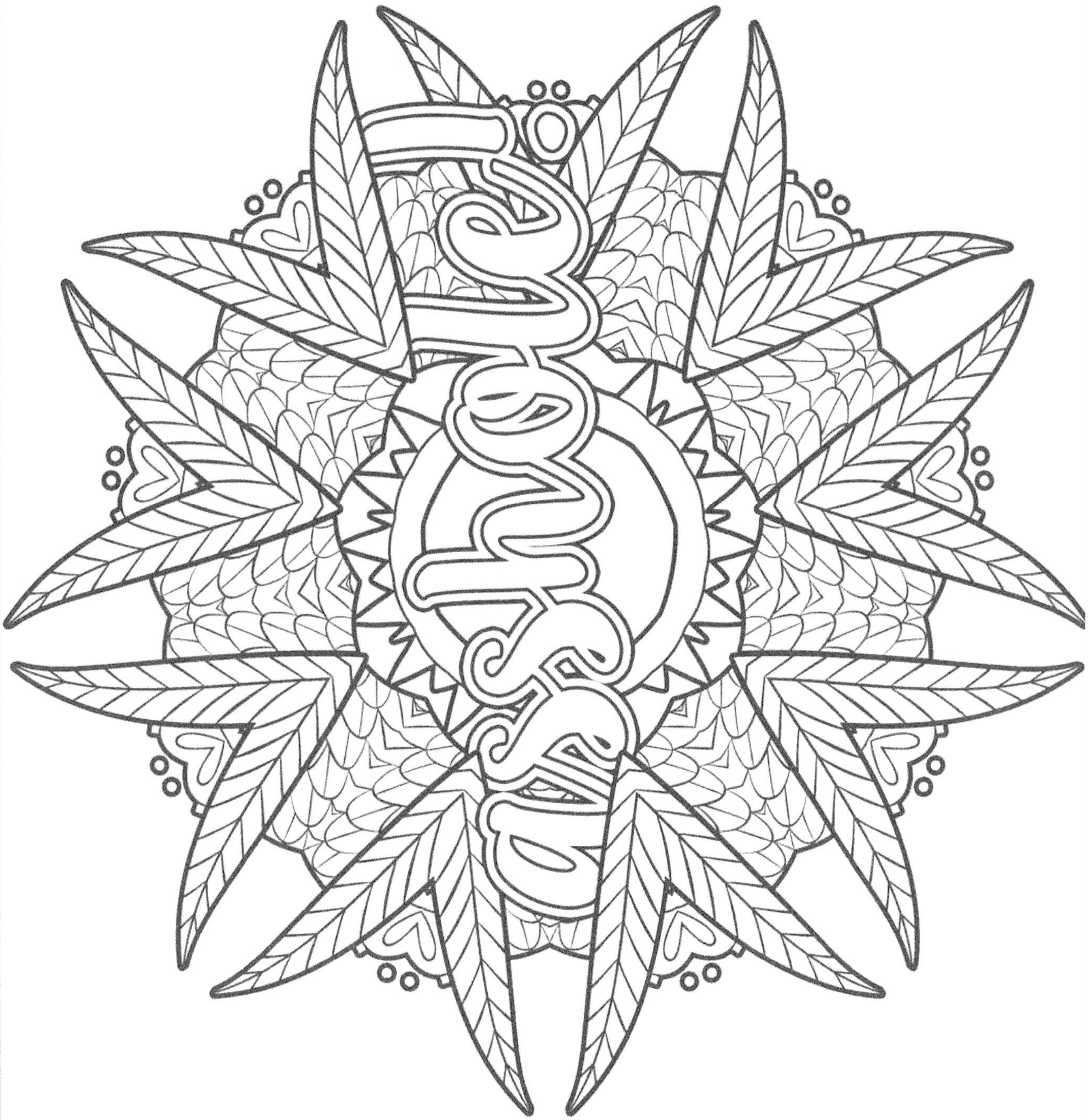
asshole!

SWEAR &
COLORS

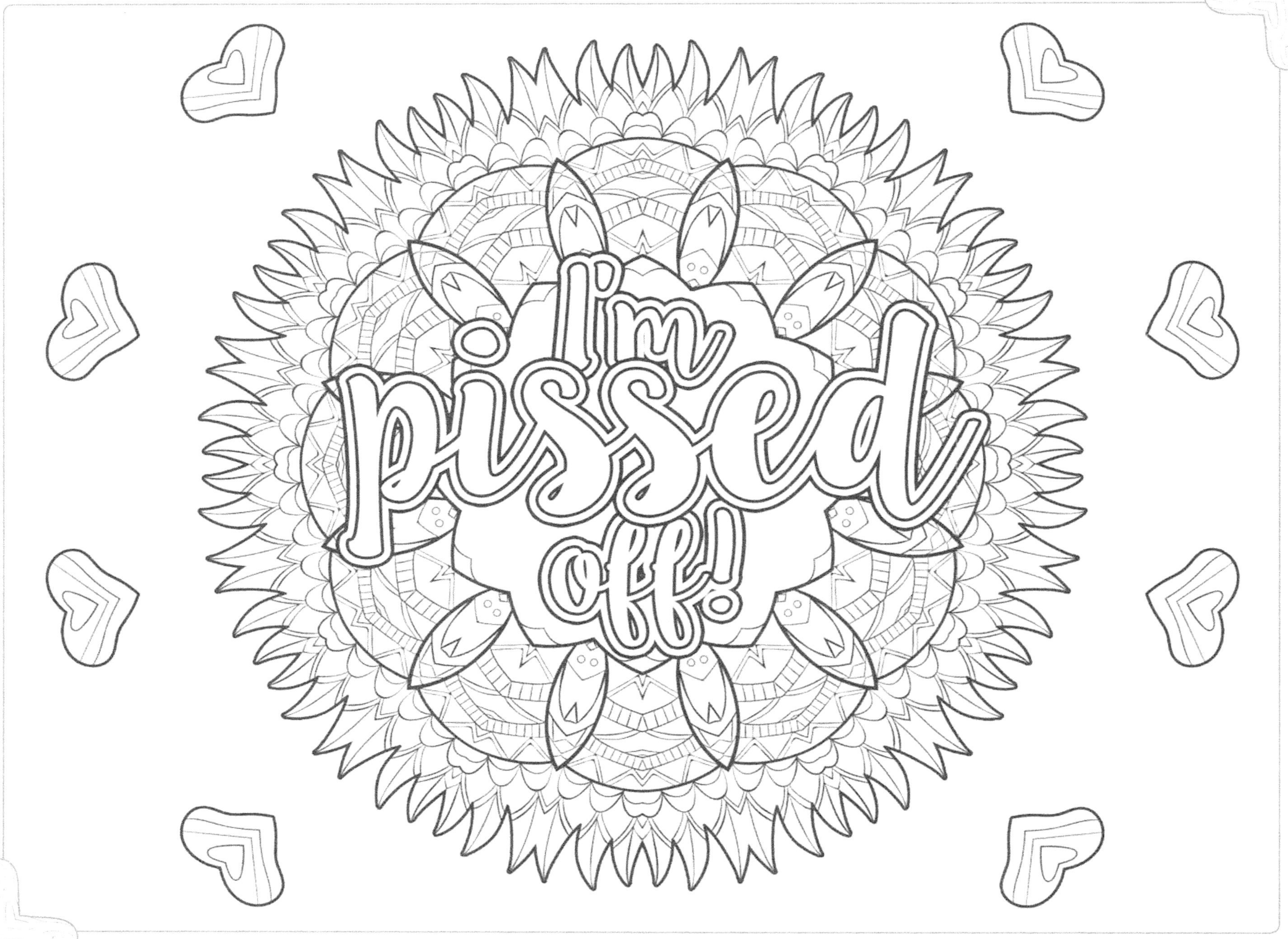
I'm pissed off!

SWEAR & COLORS

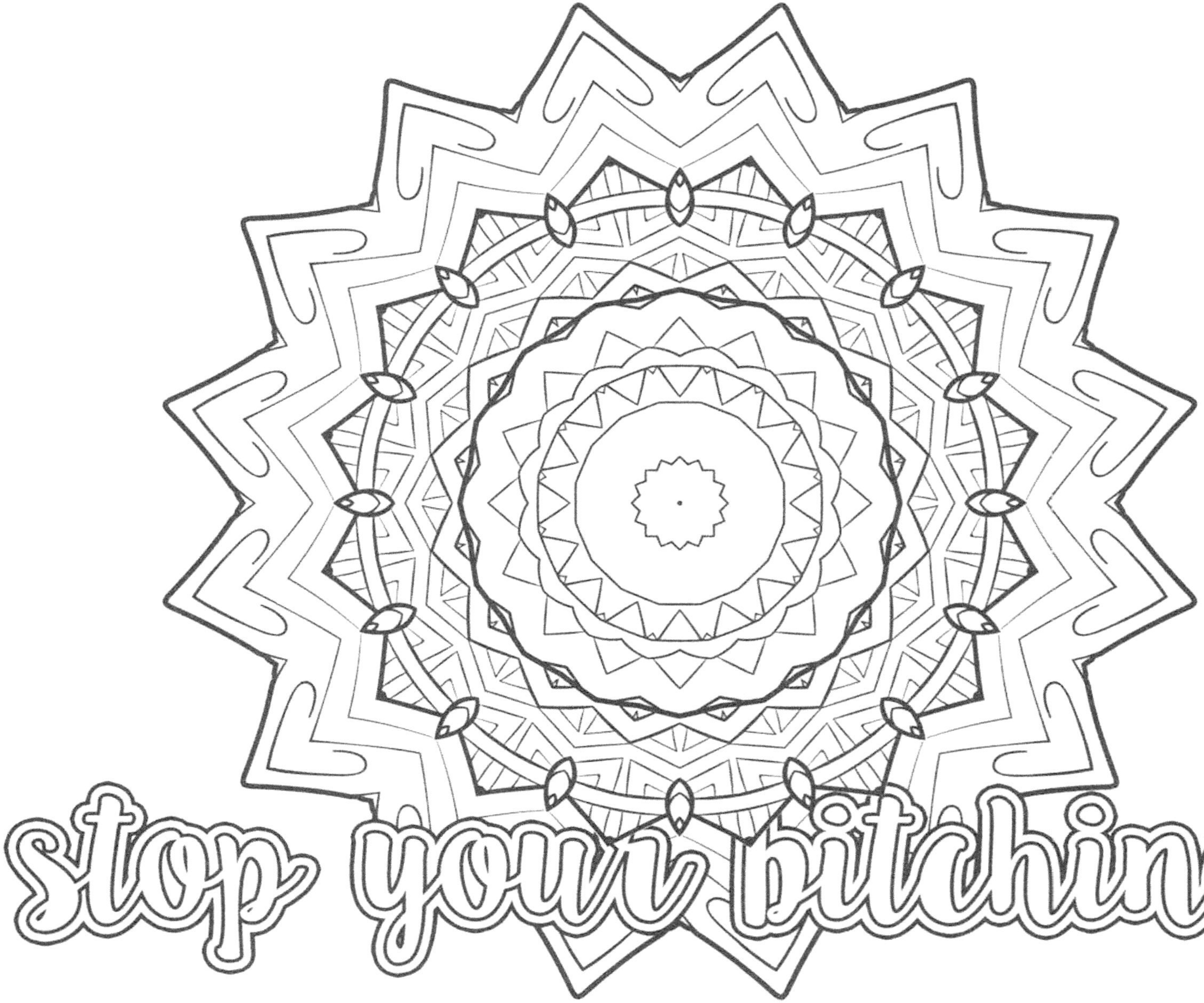
stop your bitching!

SWEAR &
COLORS

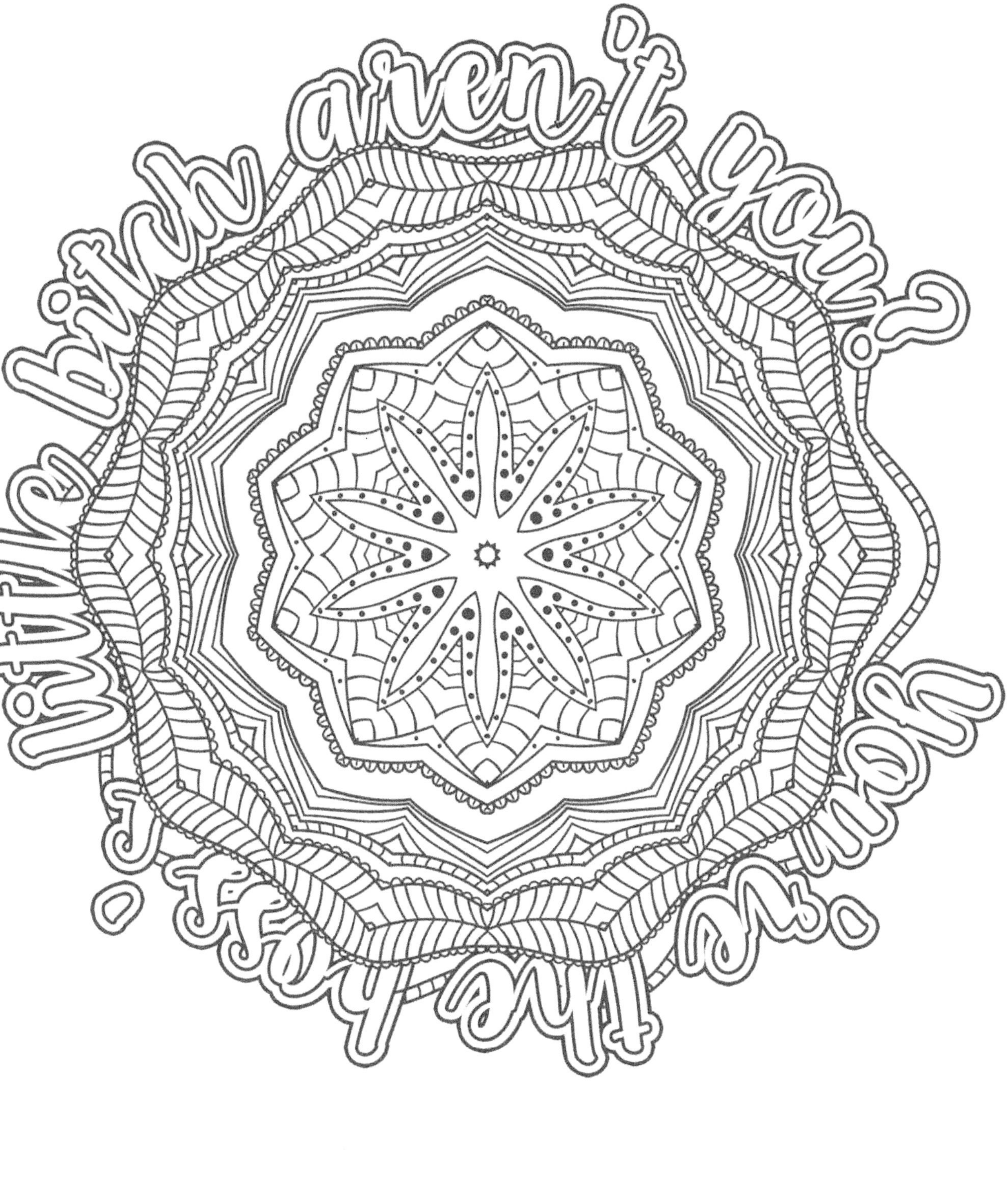
you're the boss, little bitch aren't you?

SWEAR &
COLORS

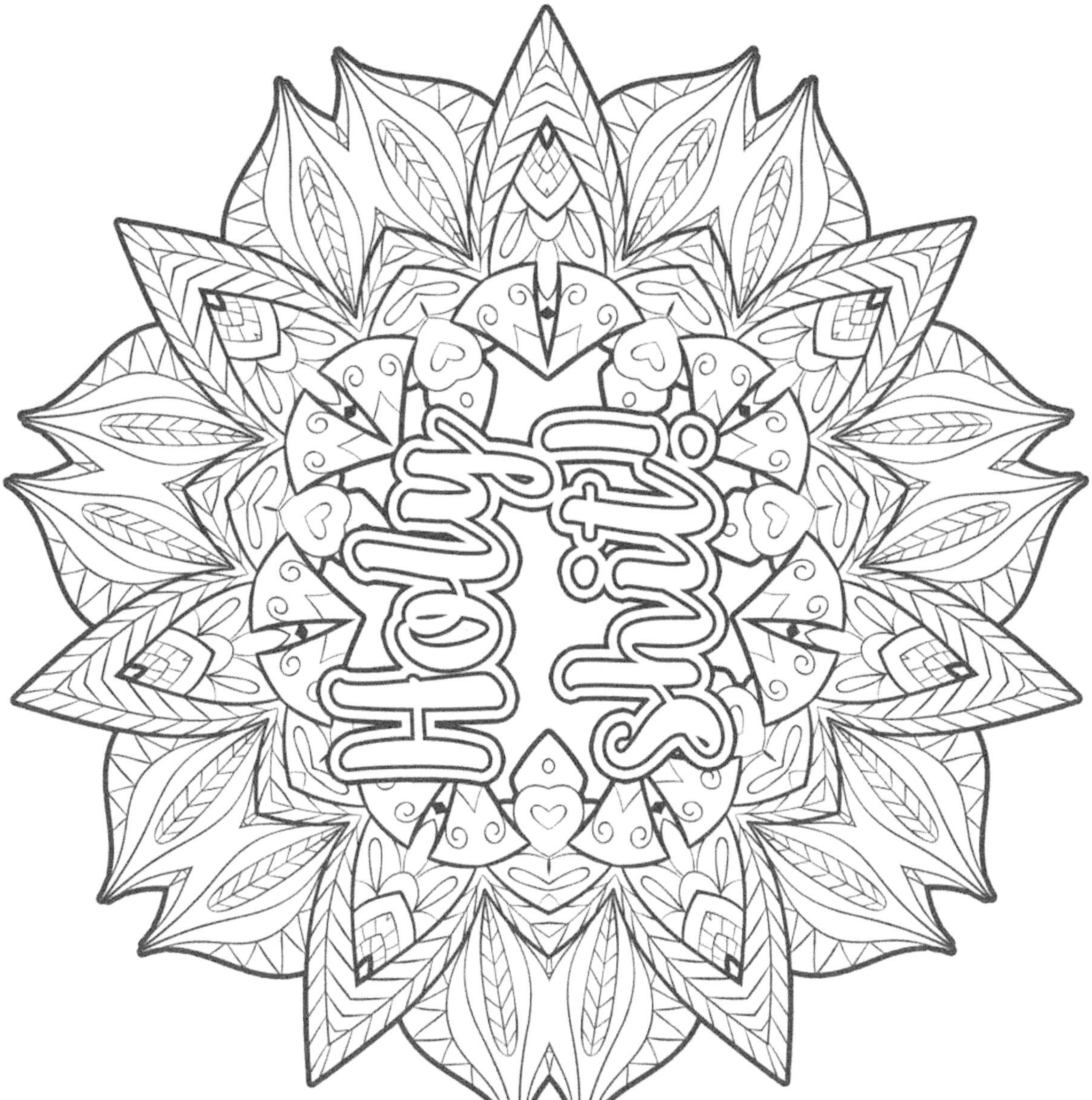
Holy Shit!

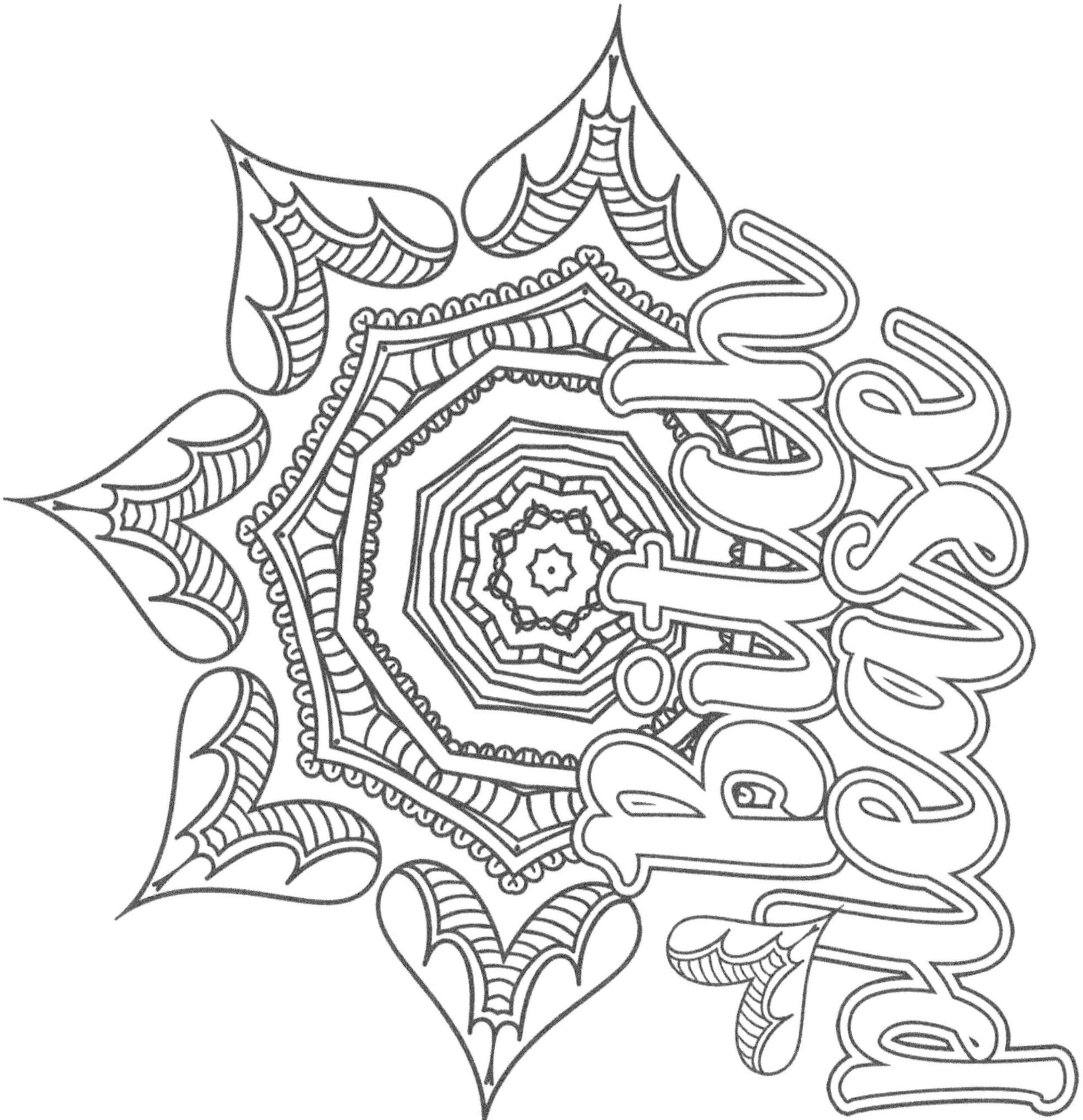
Bitch please

SWEAR &
COLORS

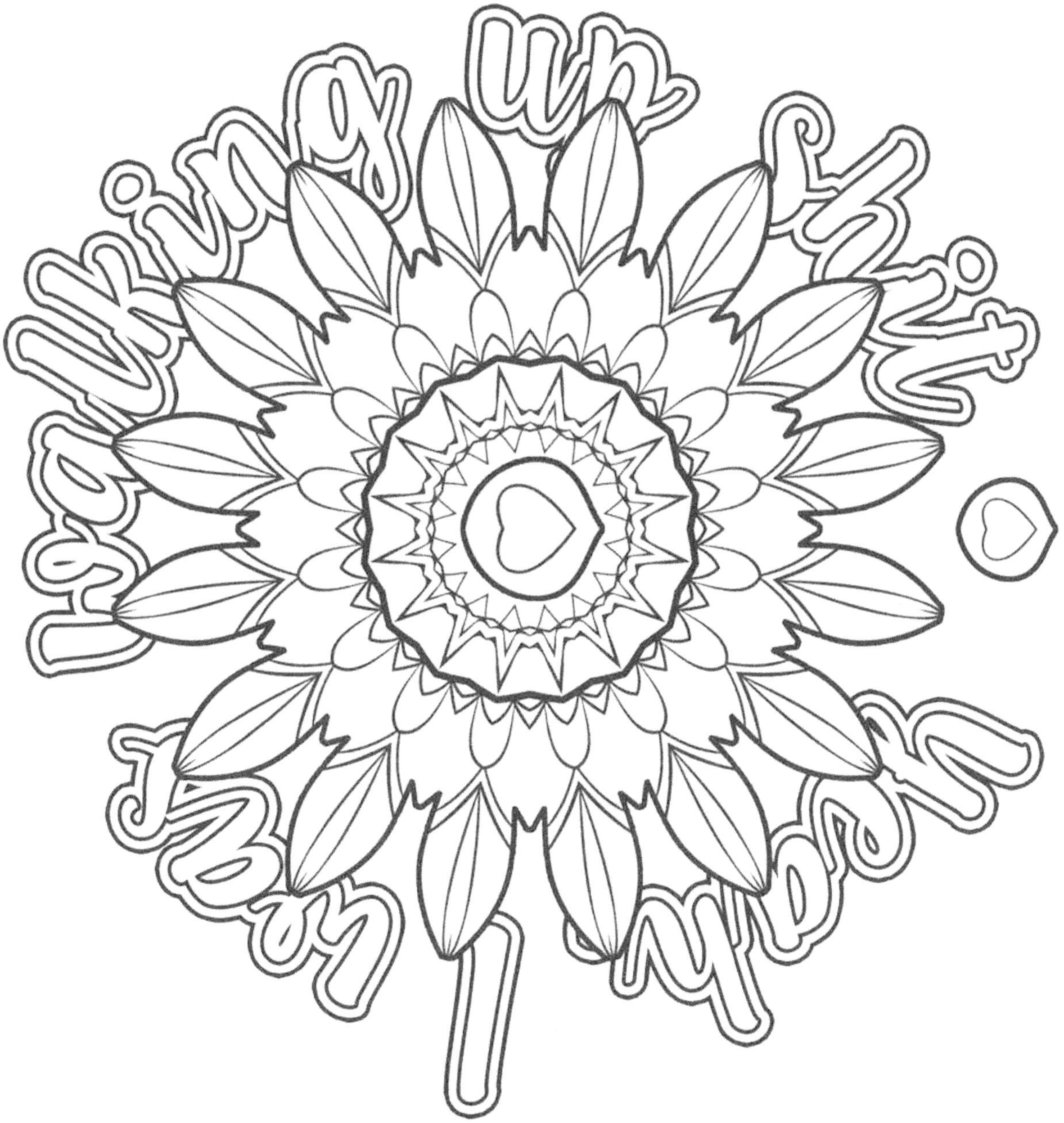
walking up shit

SWEAR & COLORS

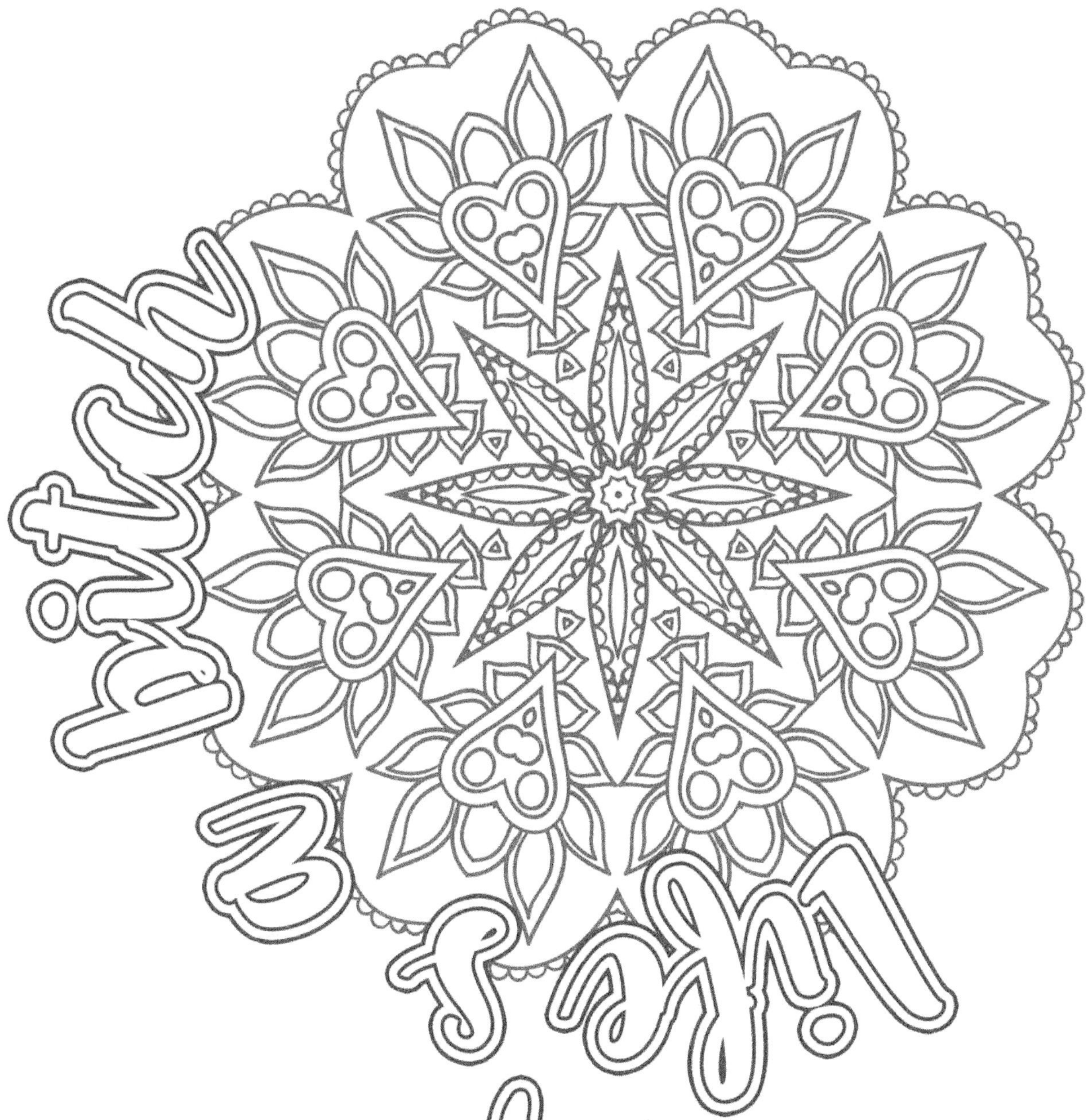
life's a bitch

SWEAR & COLORS

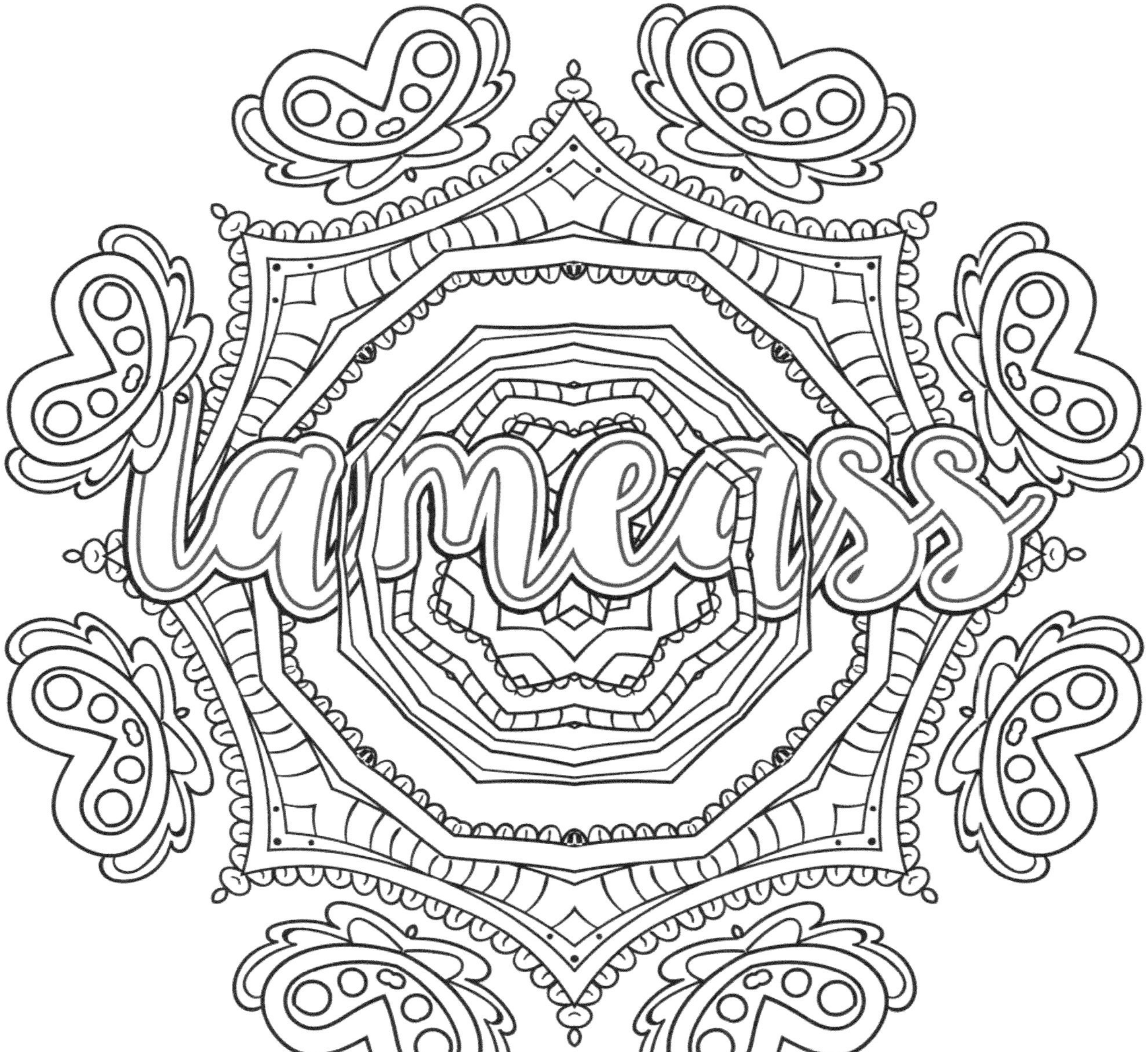
lameass

SWEAR&
COLORS

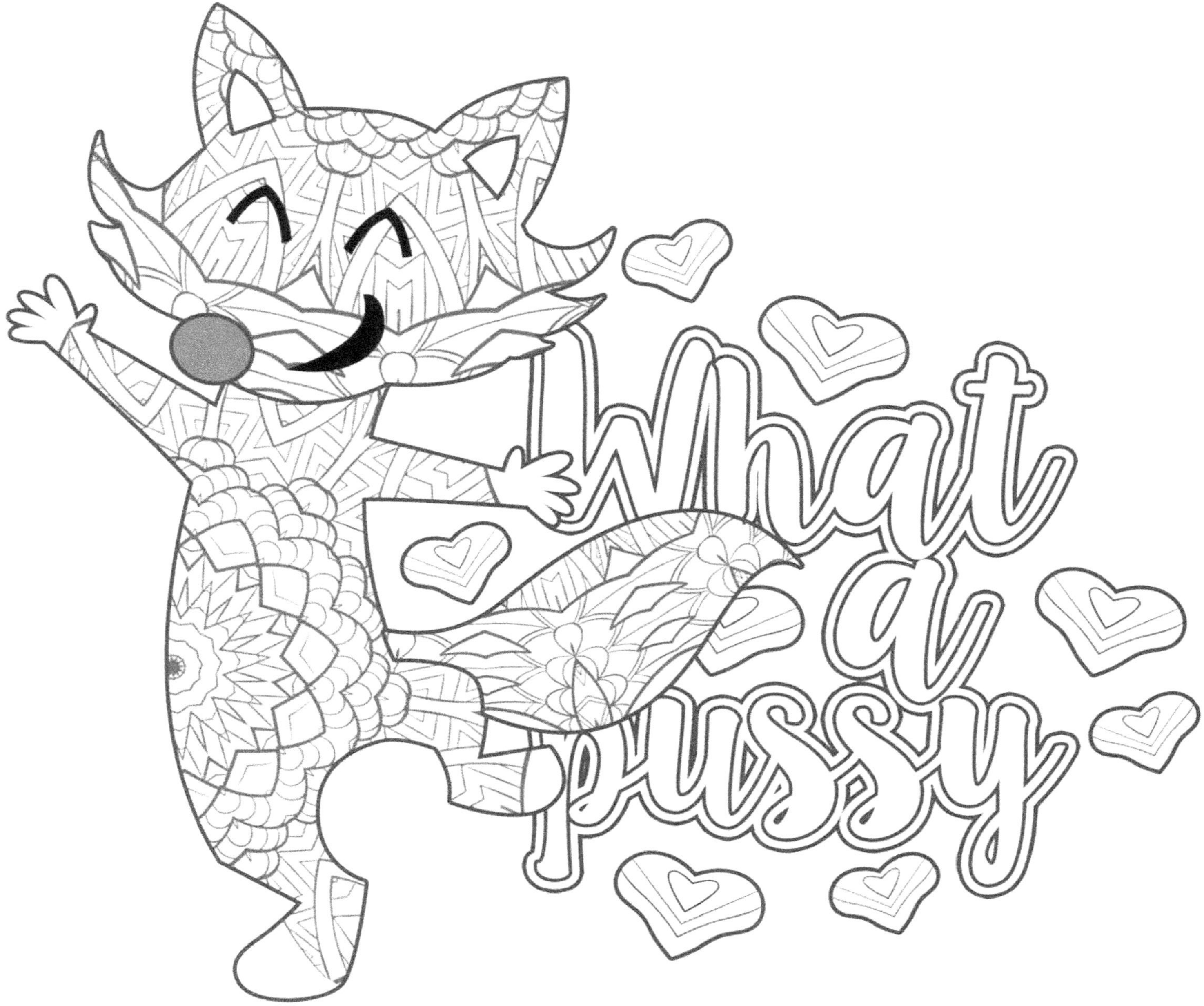
What a pussy

SWEAR & COLORS

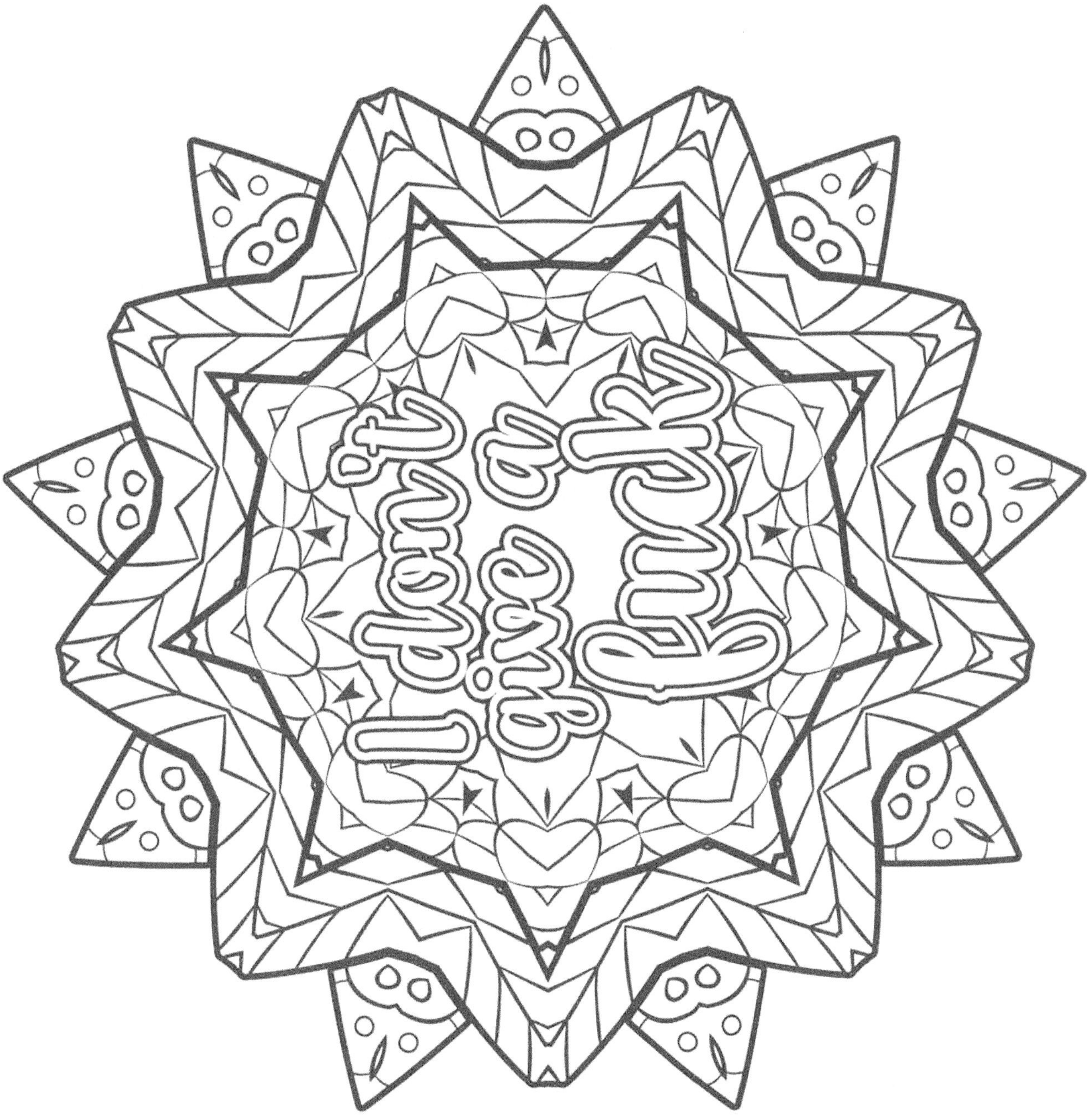
I don't
give a
fuck

SWEAR &
COLORS

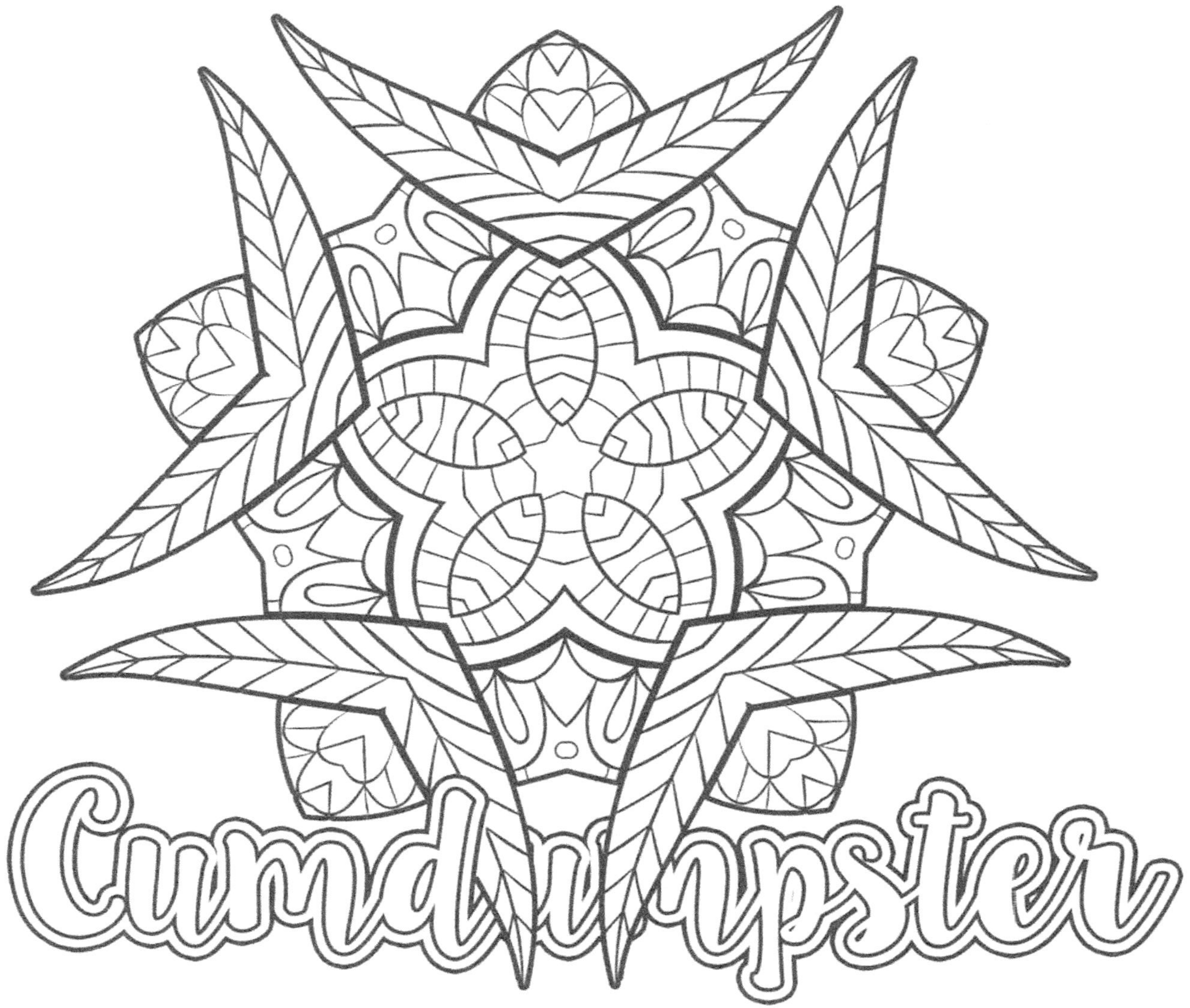
Cumdumpster

SWEAR &
COLORS

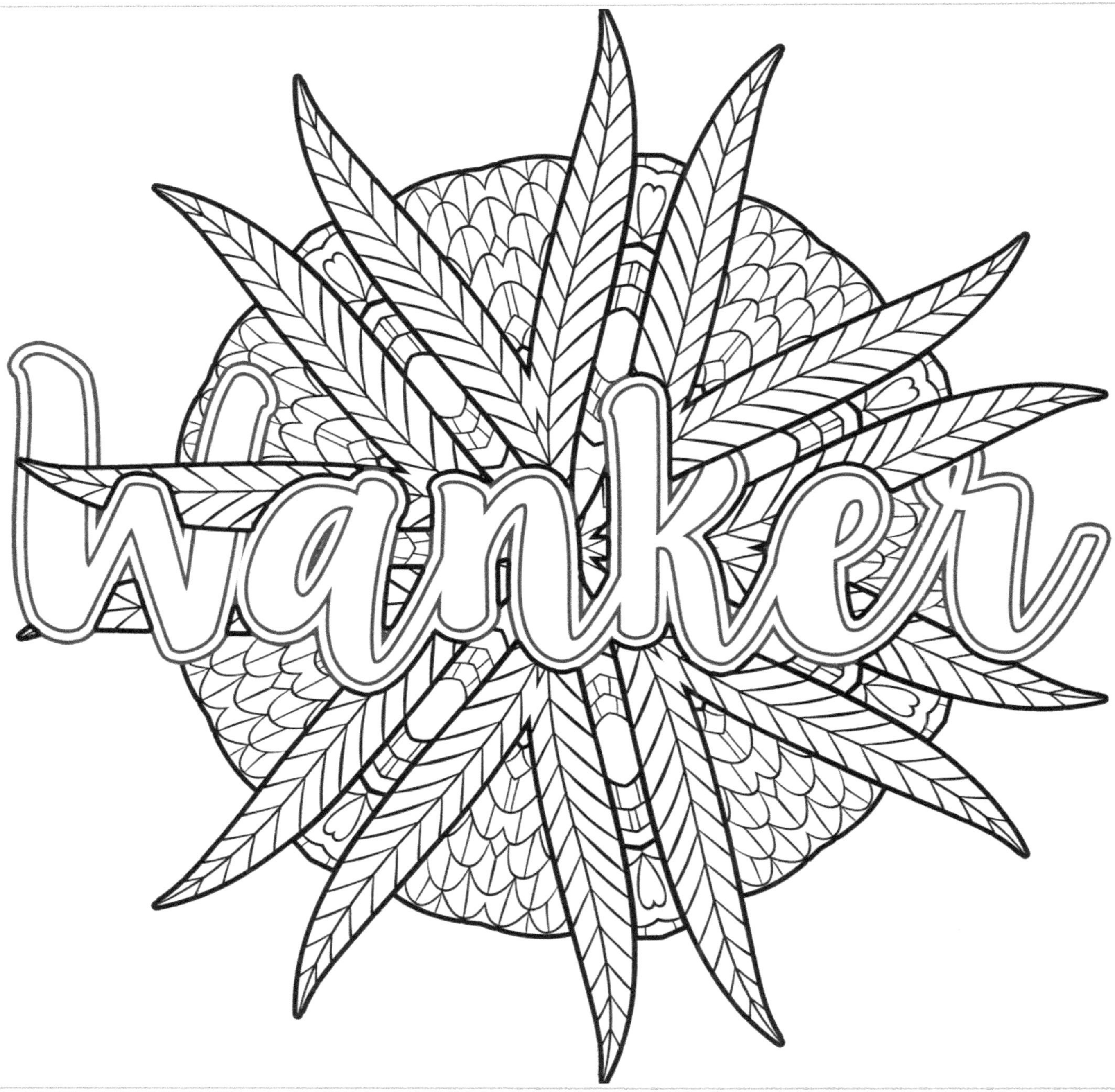
Wanker

SWEAR & COLORS

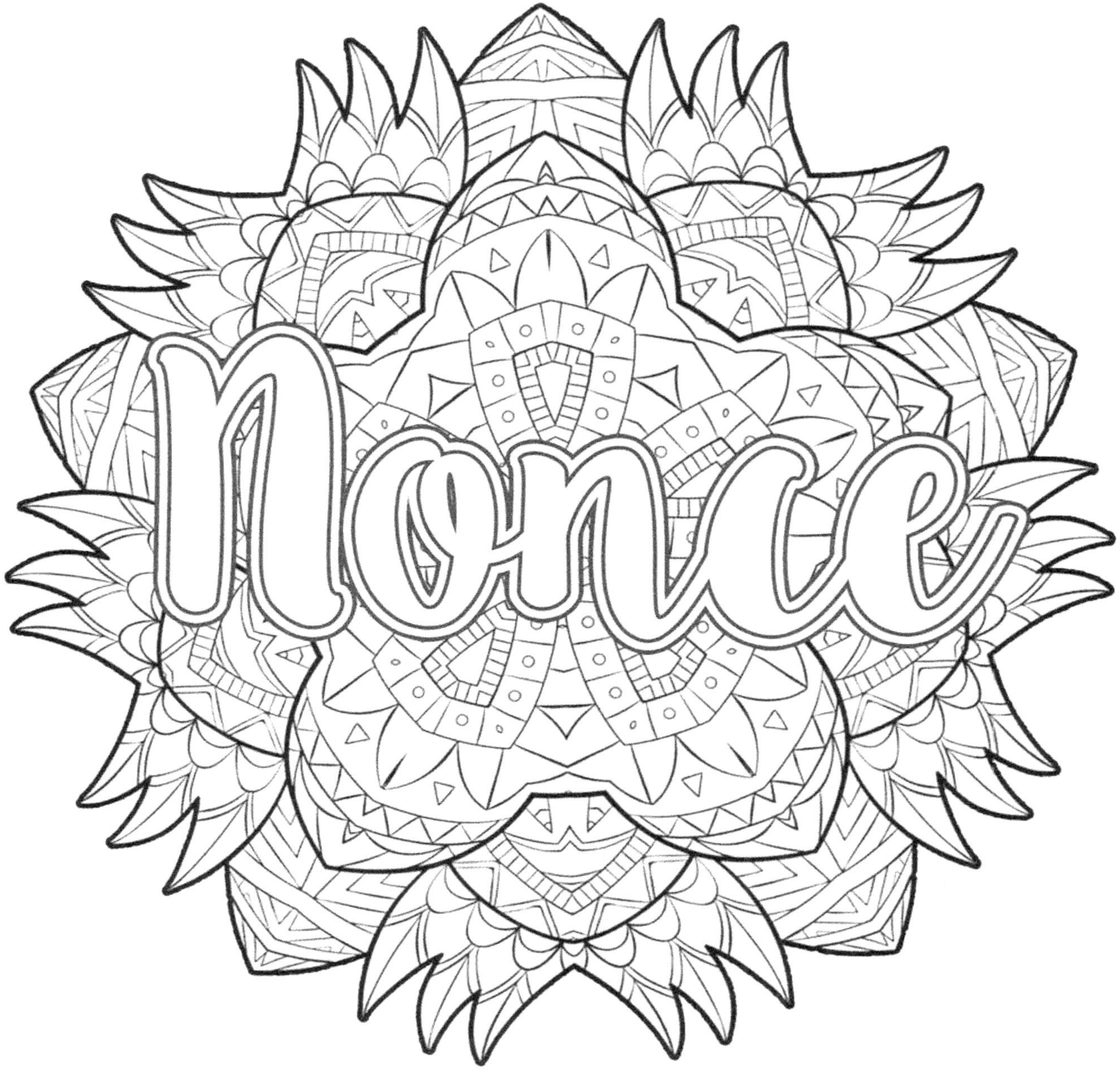
Nonce

SWEAR & COLORS

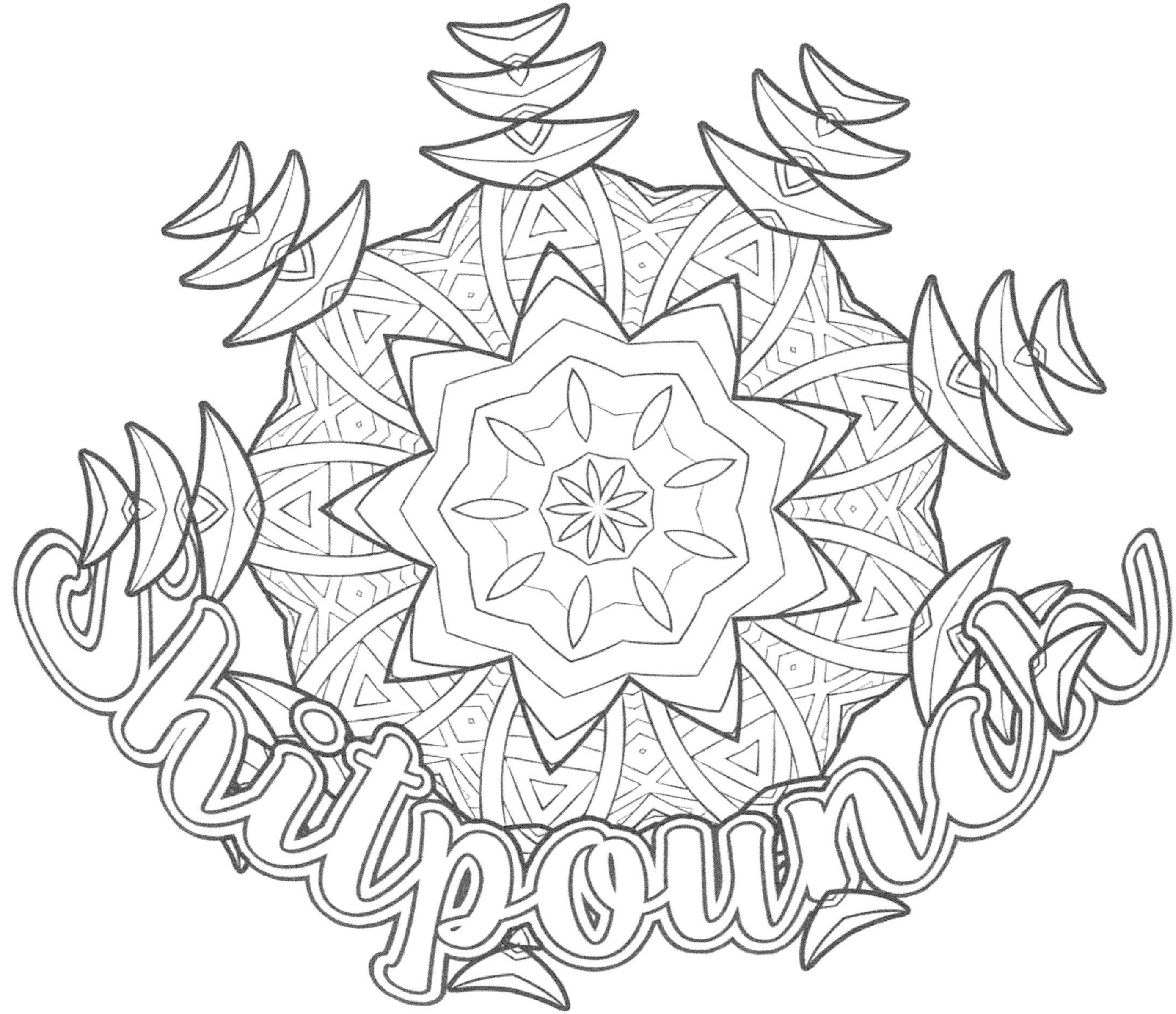
Shitpouncer

SWEAR & COLORS

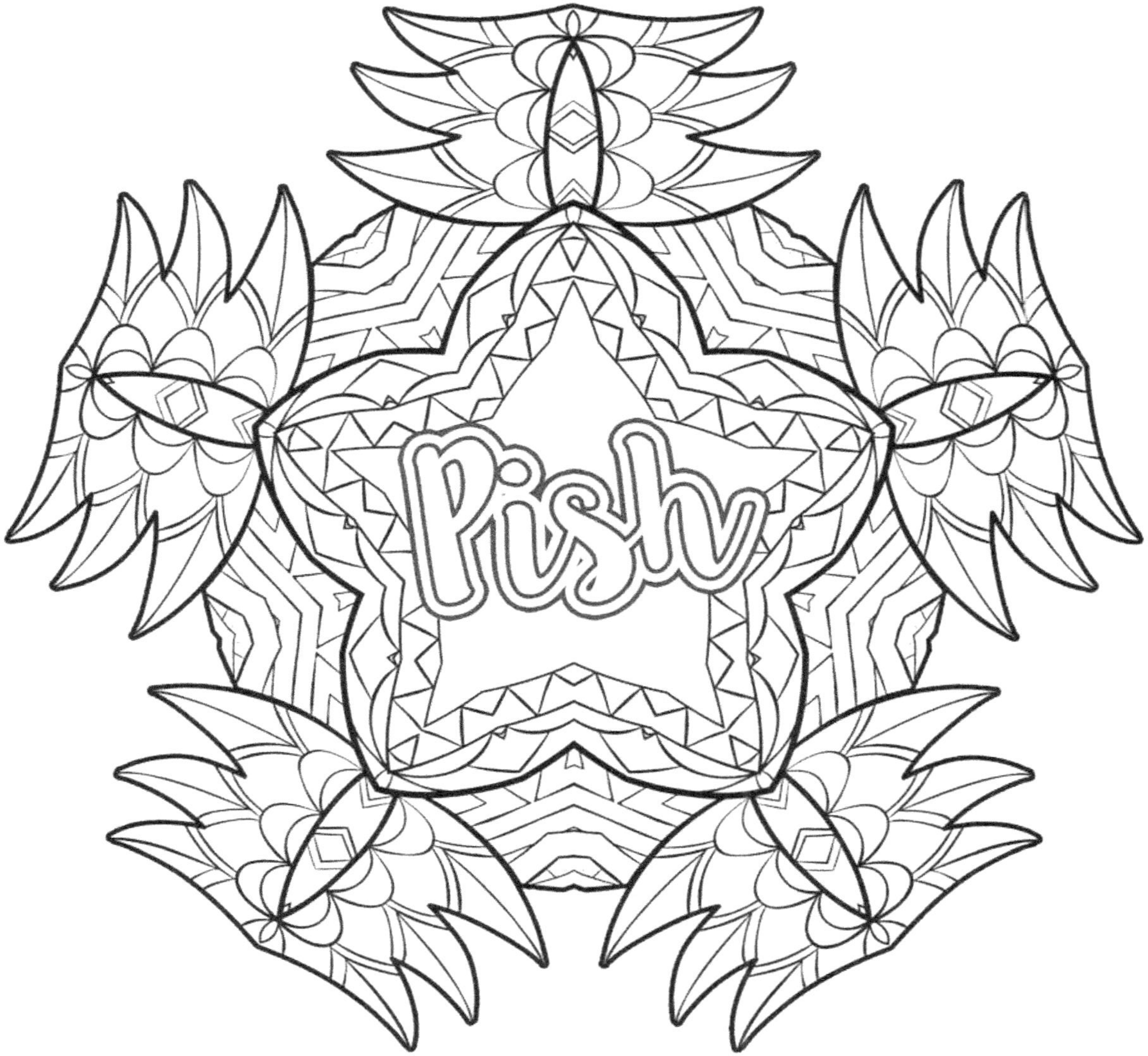
Pish

SWEAR & COLORS

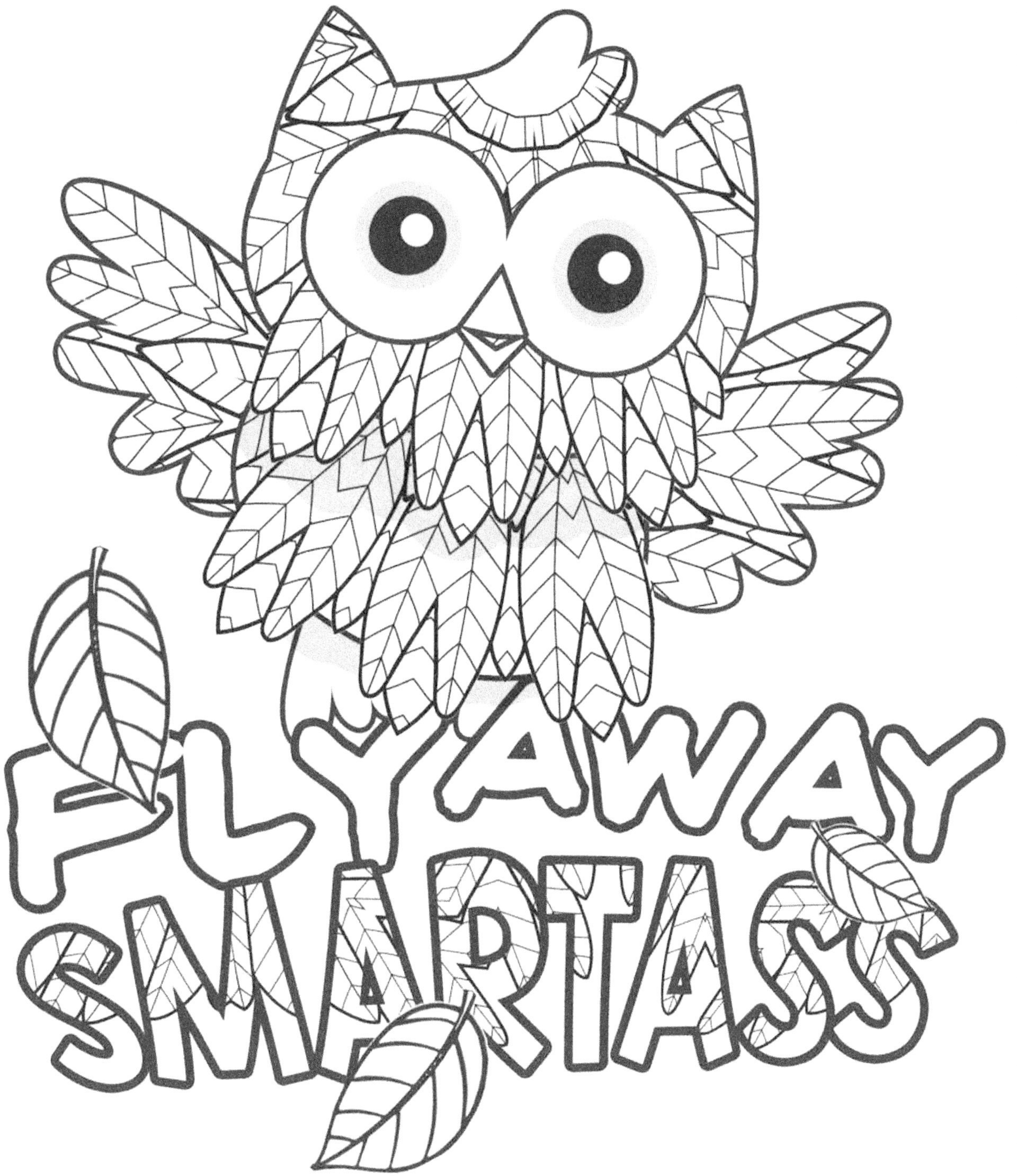
FLY AWAY
SMARTASS

SWEAR & COLORS

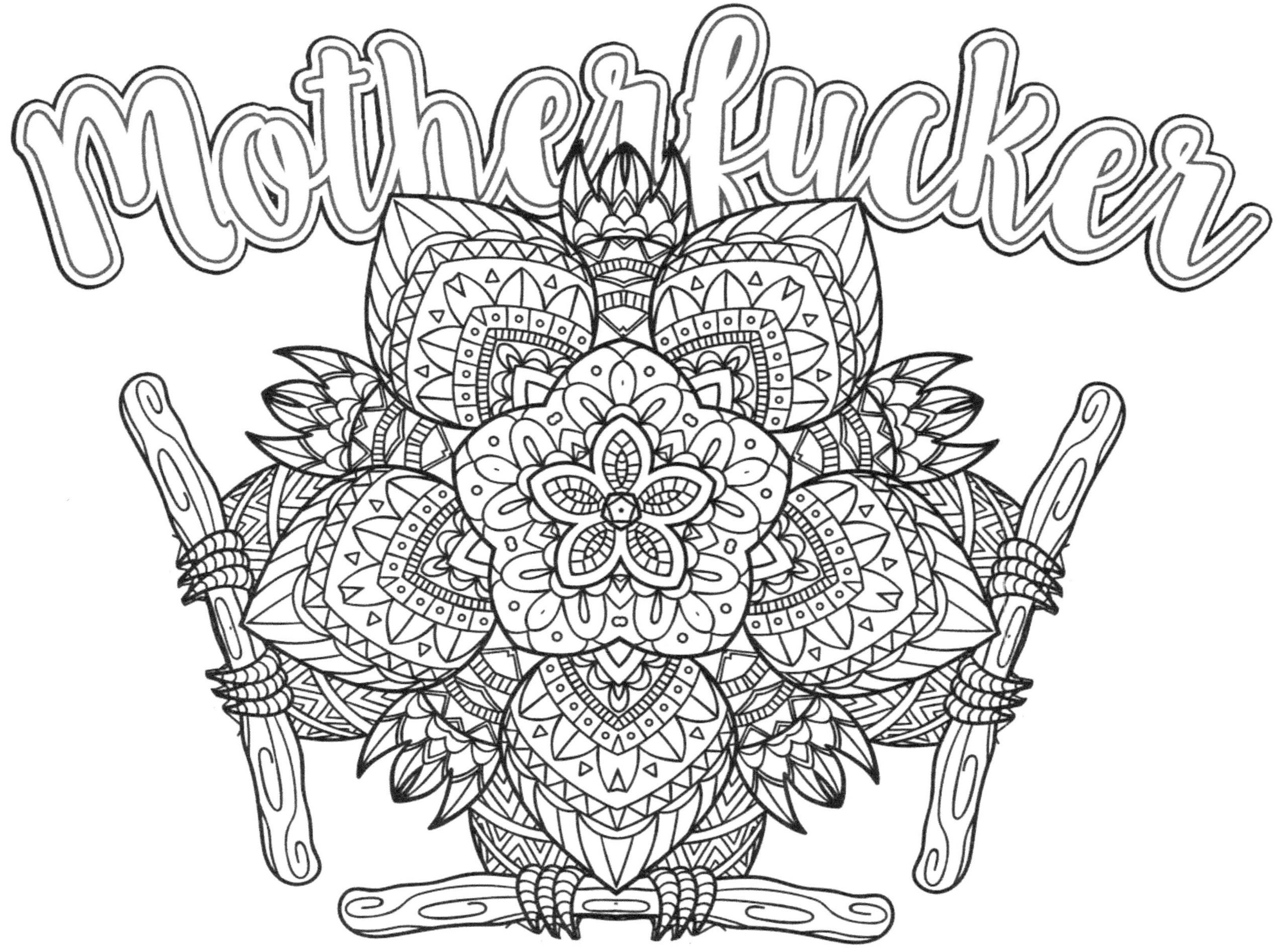
Motherfucker

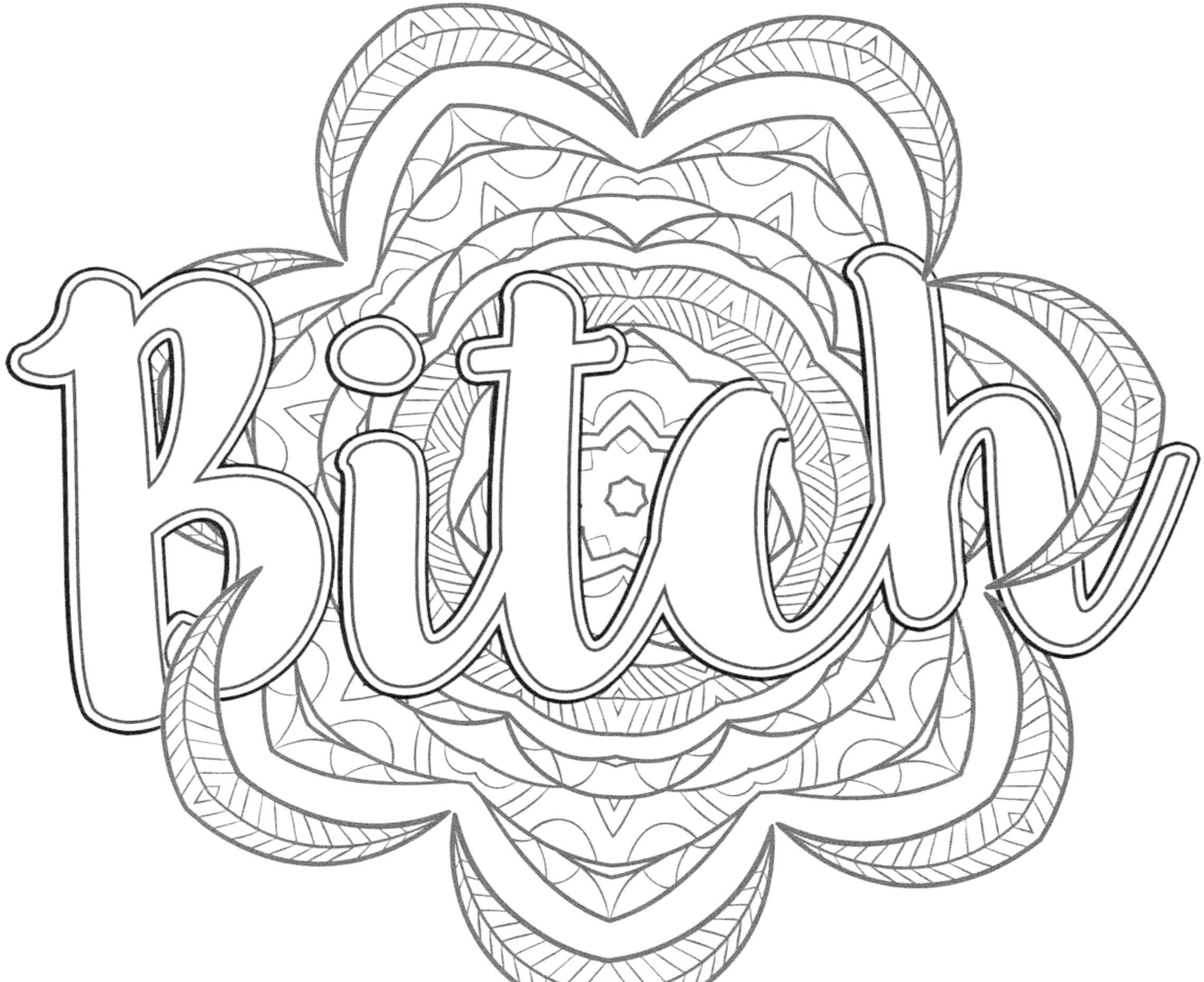
Bitch

SWEAR & COLORS

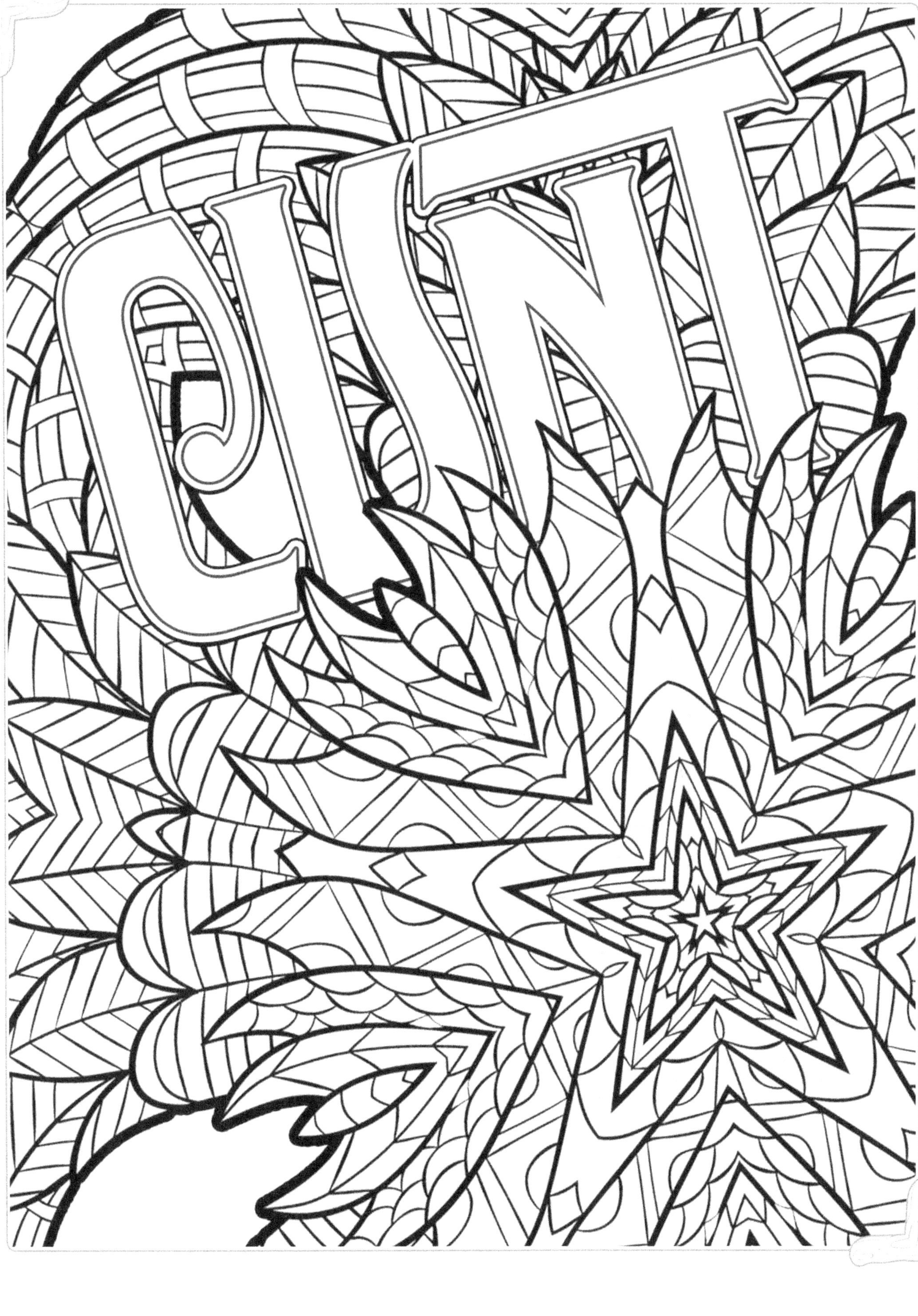
CUNT

SWEAR &
COLORS

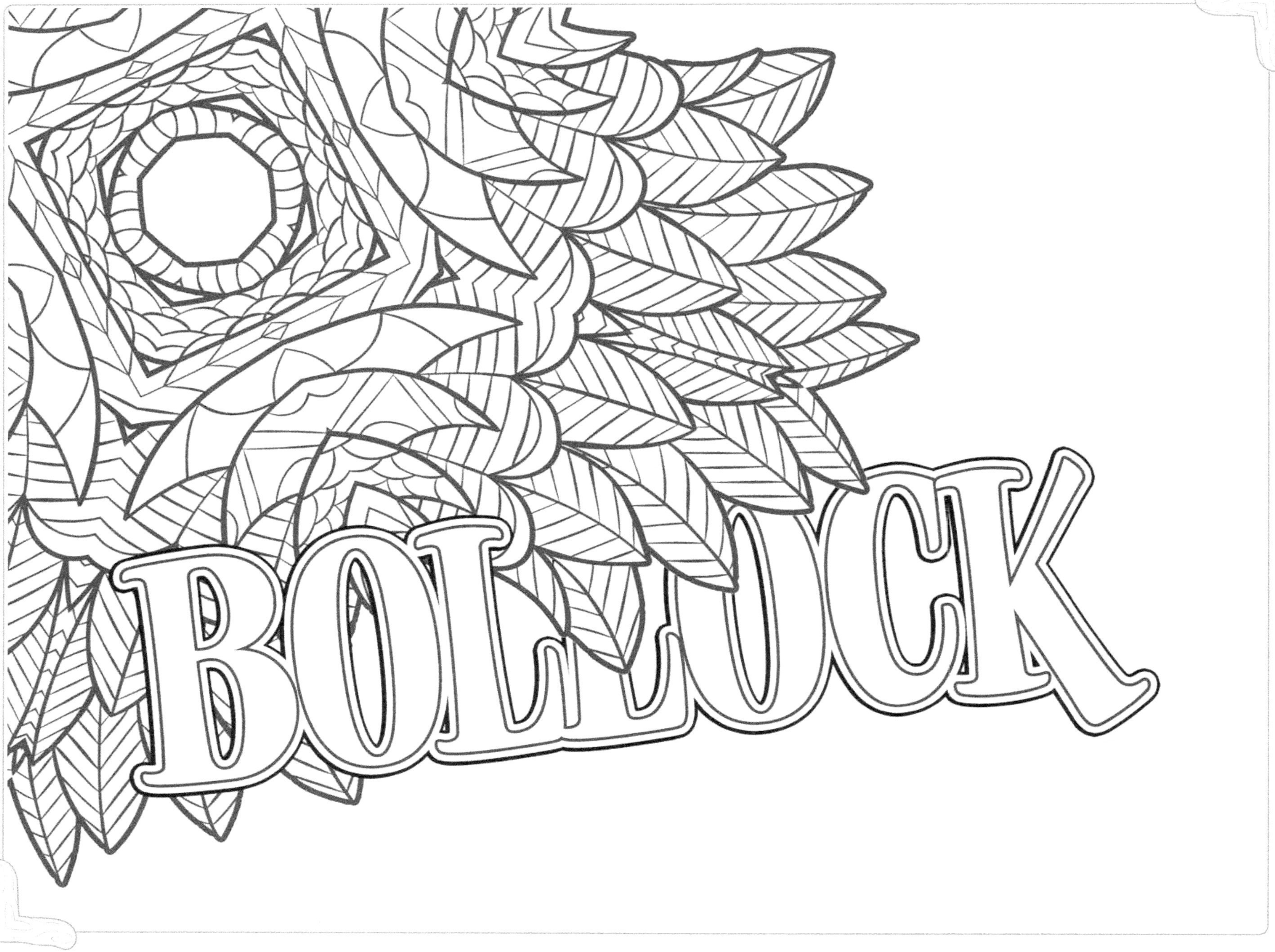
BOLLOCK

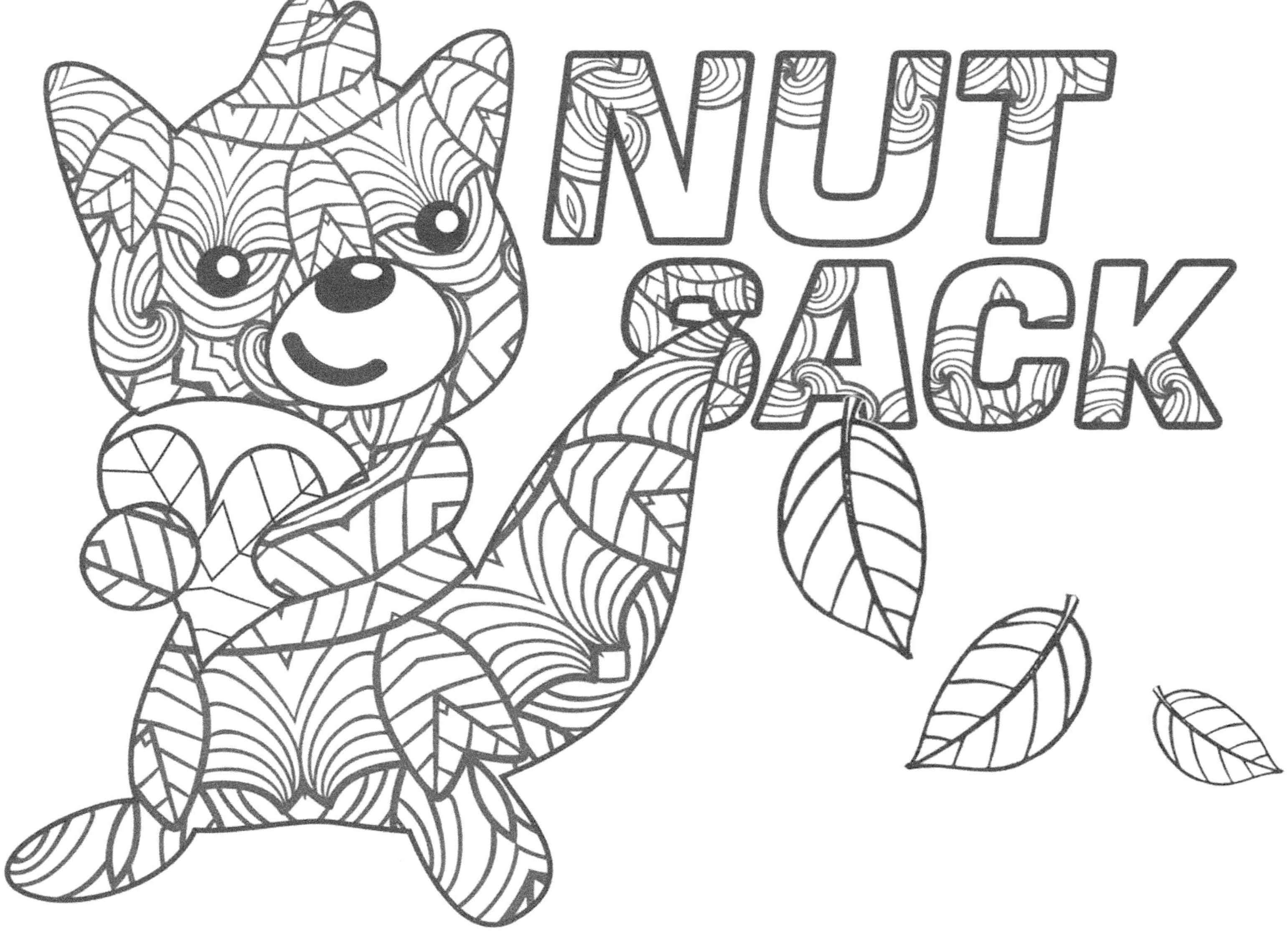
NUT
SACK

SWEAR & COLORS

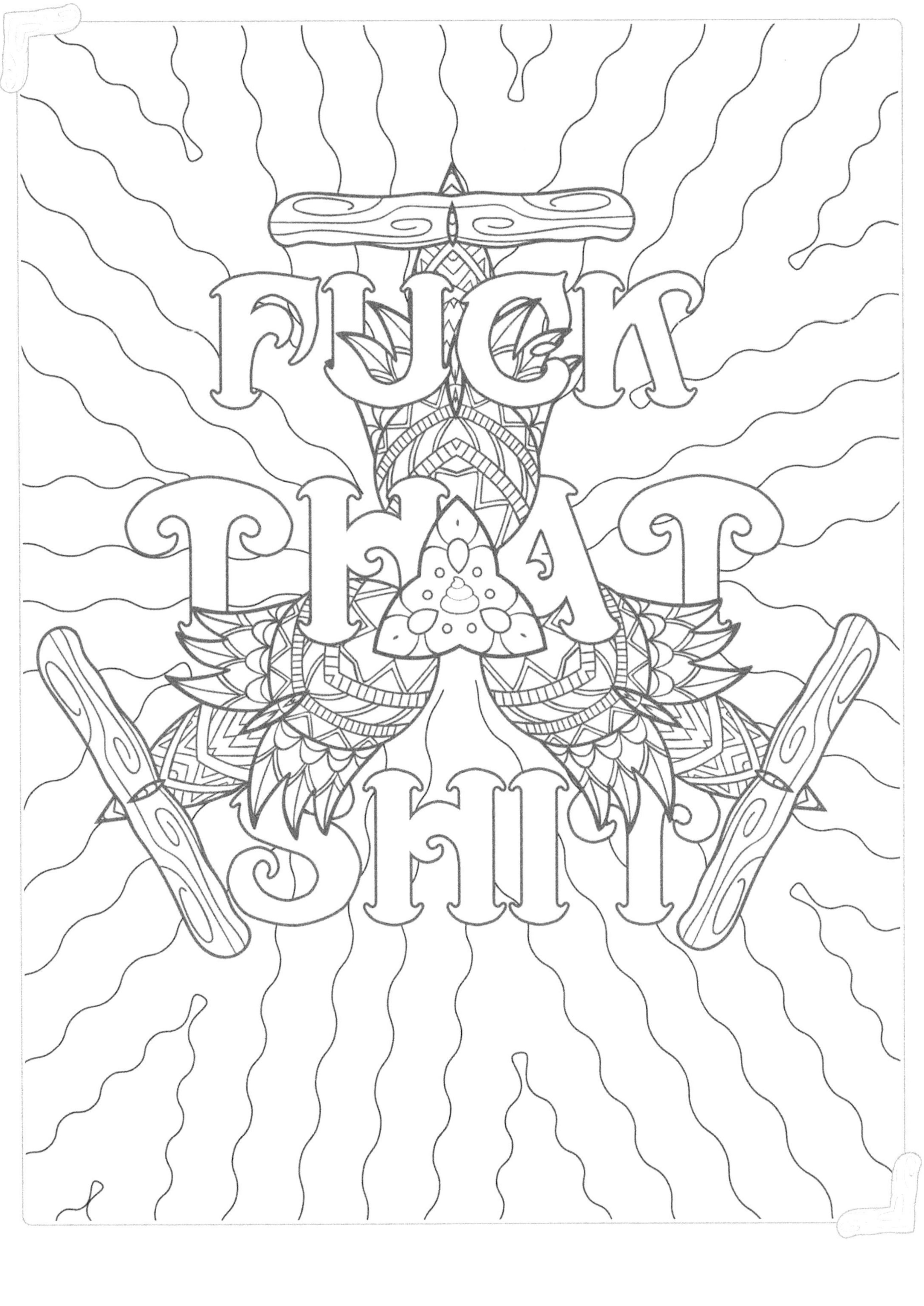
FUCK
THAT
SHIT

SWEAR & COLORS

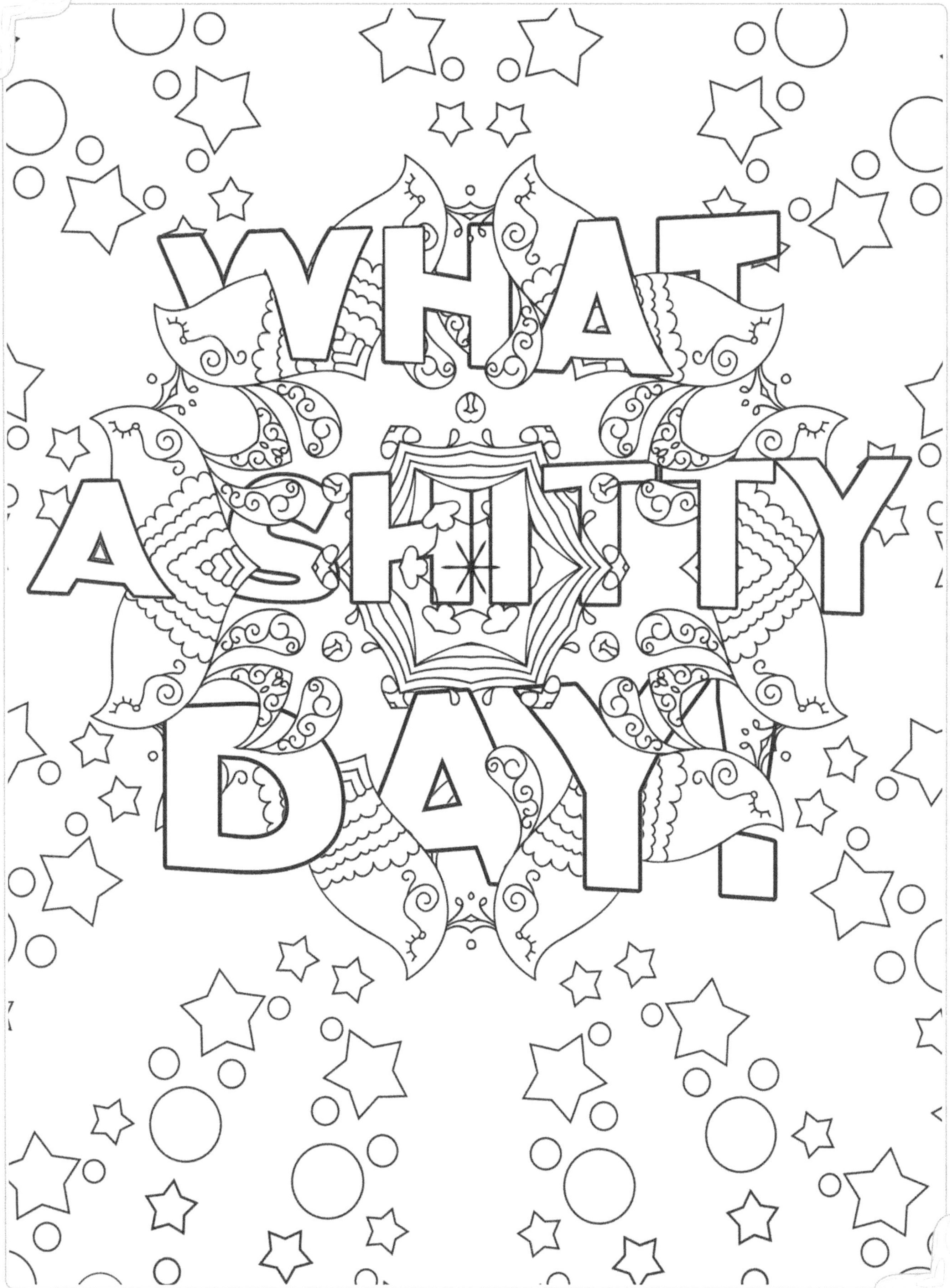
WHAT
A SHITTY
DAY!

SWEAR & COLORS

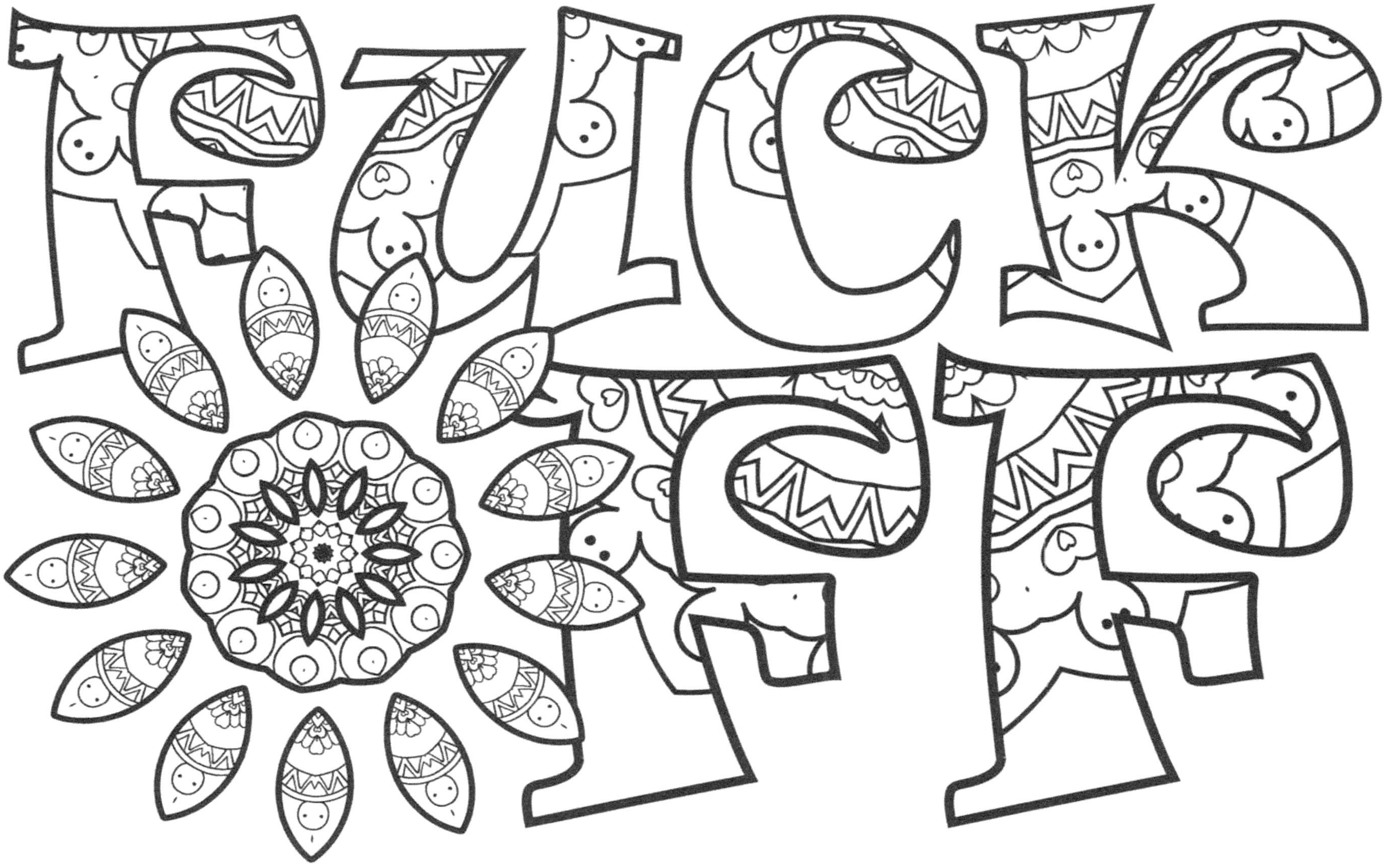
Fuck
off

SWEAR&
COLORS

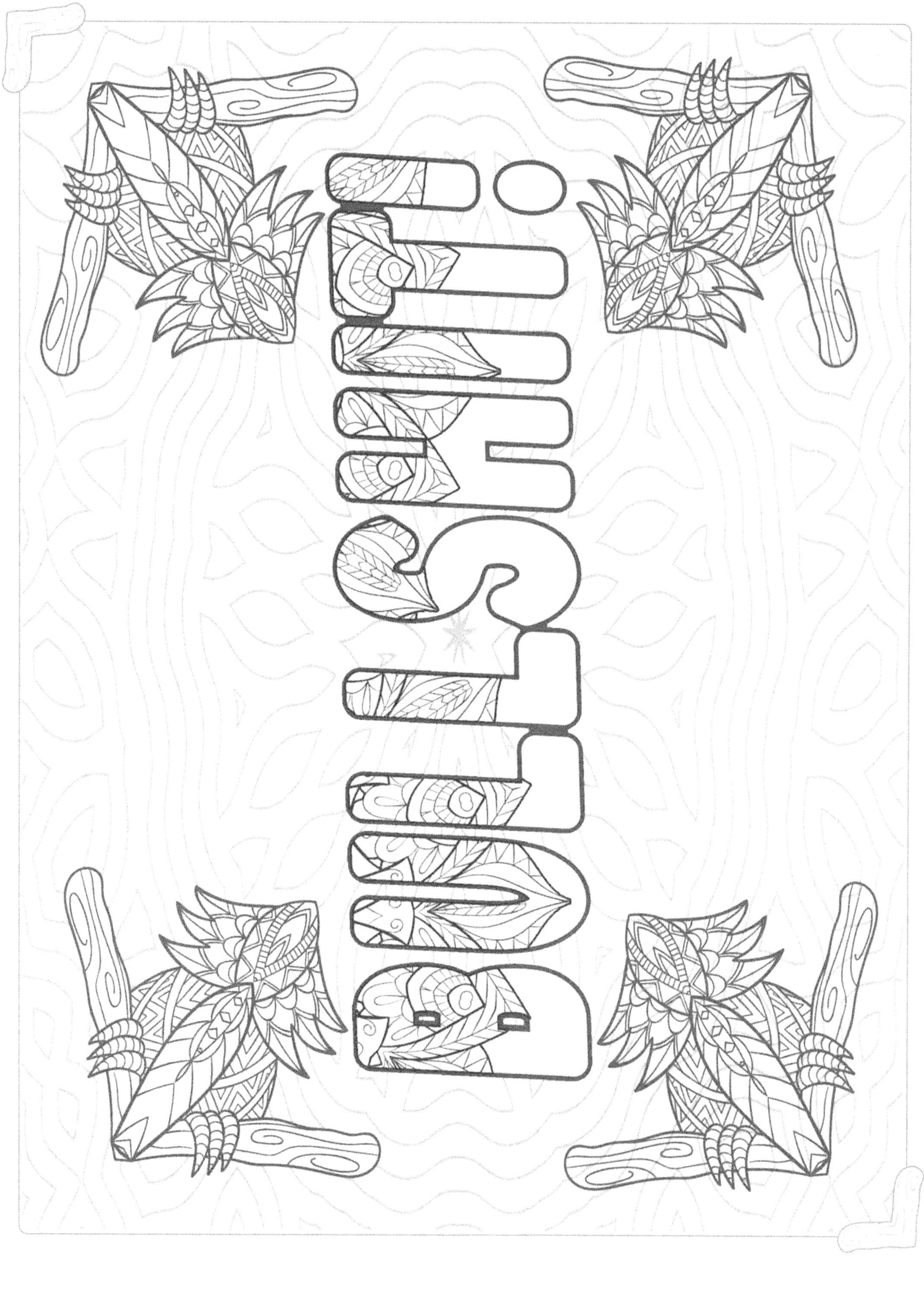
BULLSHIT!

SWEAR &
COLORS

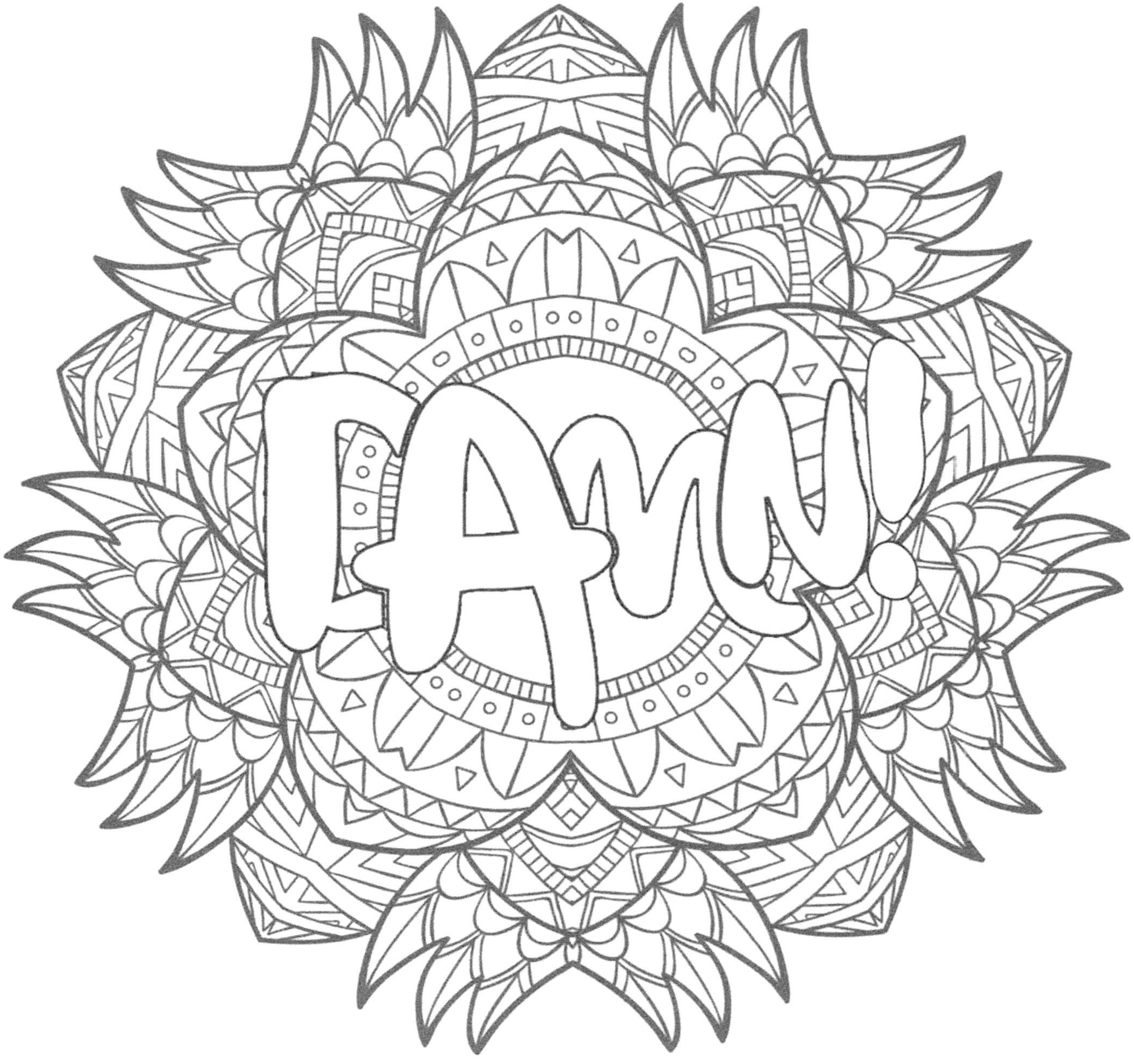
DAMN!

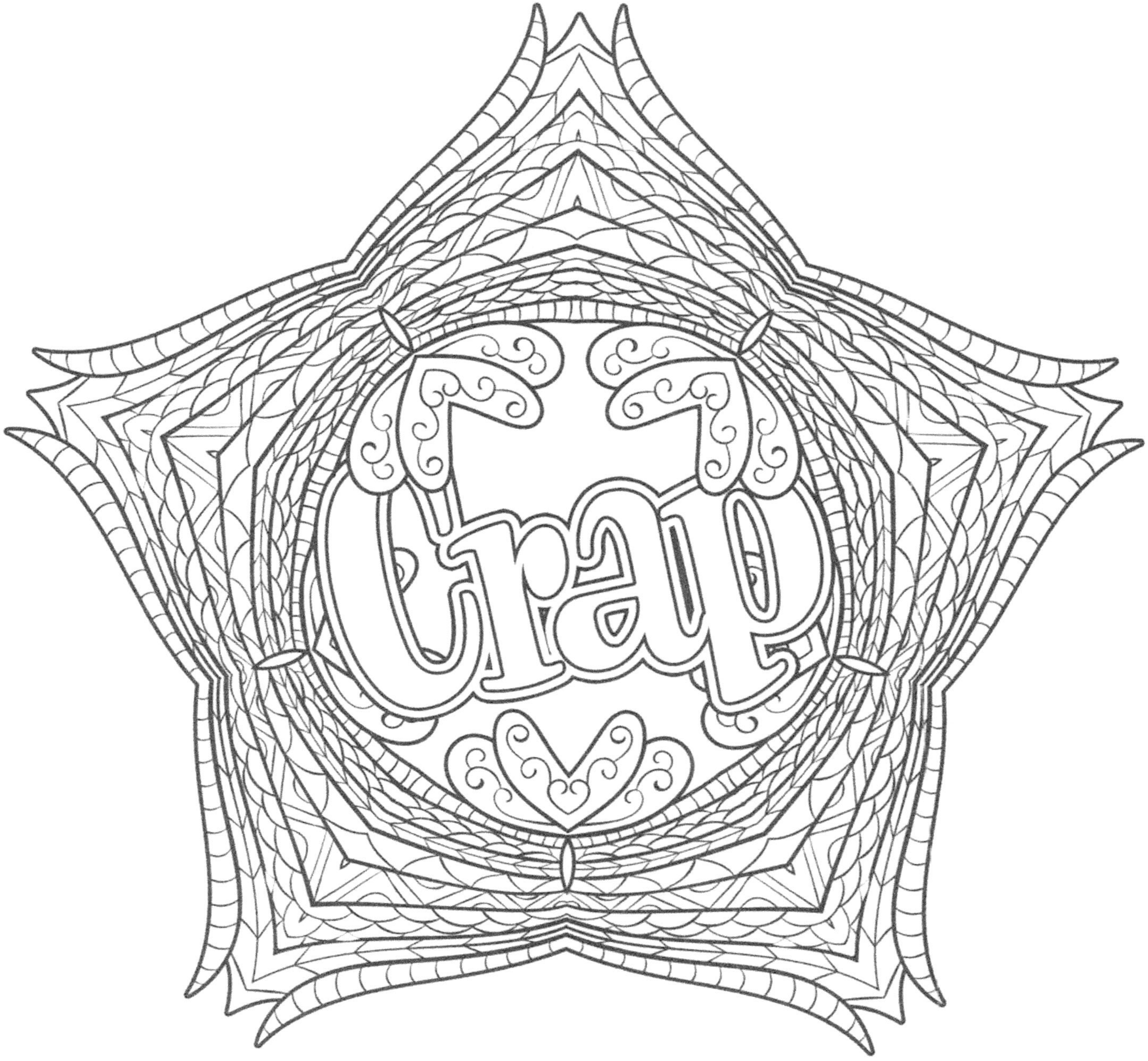
Crap

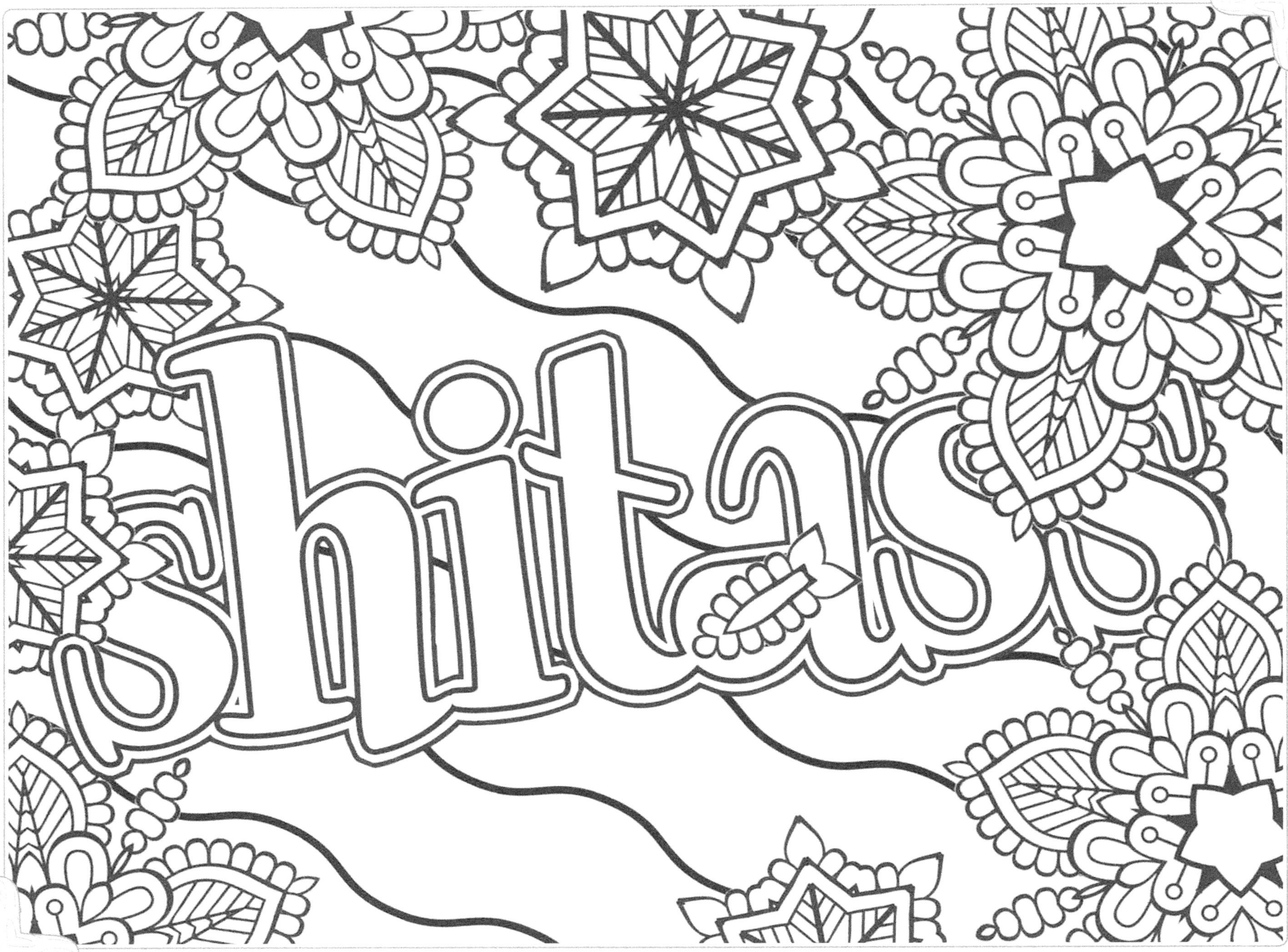
shitass

SWEAR & COLORS

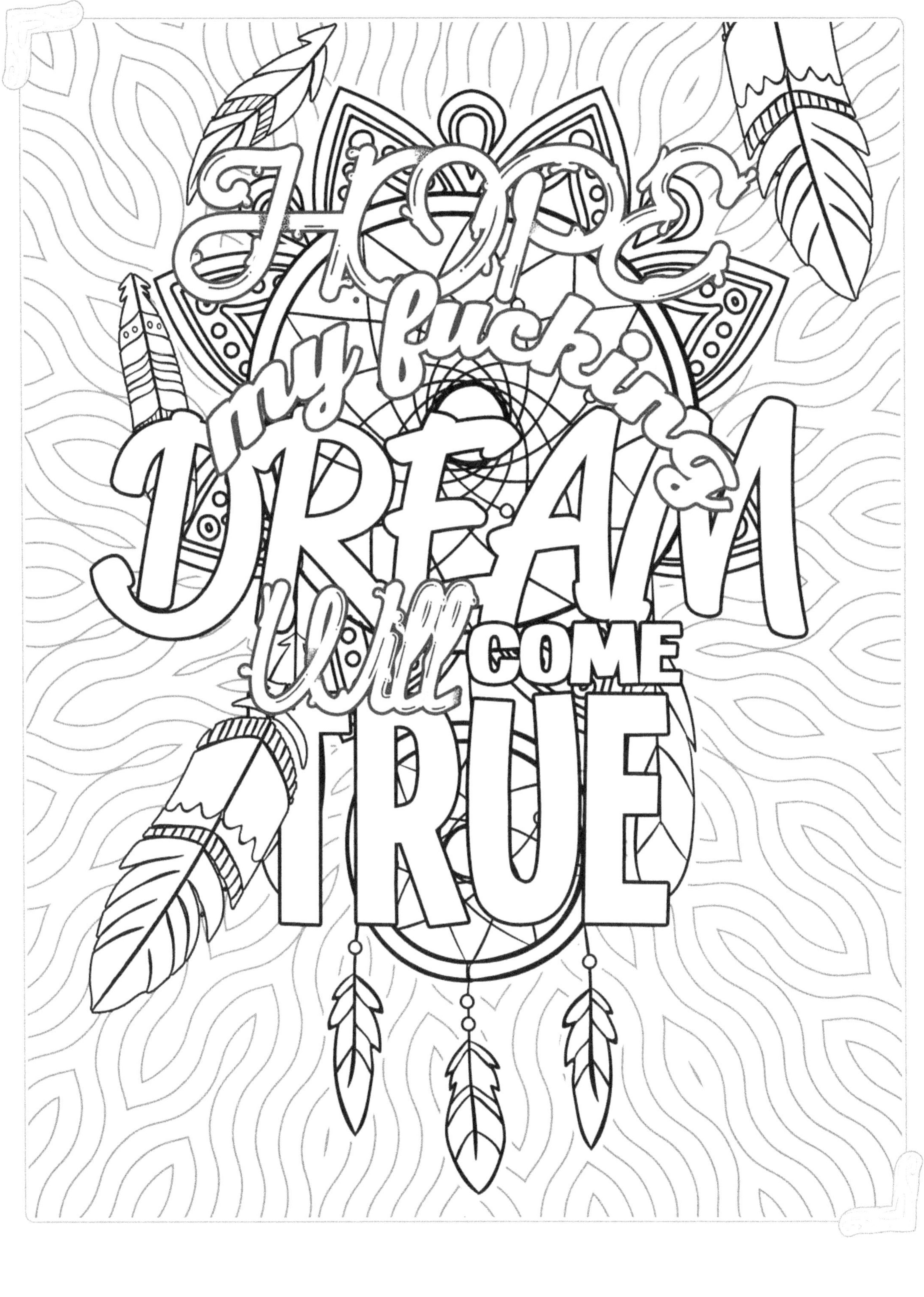
Hope
my fucking
DREAM
will come
TRUE

SWEAR &
COLORS

www.ingramcontent.com/pod-product-compliance
Lightning Source LLC
Chambersburg PA
CBHW081119180526
45170CB00008B/2924
* 9 7 8 1 5 3 9 7 2 4 6 1 2 *